The Chief Financial Office and Corporate Performance

Financial management encompasses a set of complex activities that should be performed by a professional financial manager. Some financial decisions are riskier than others, and as such can result in higher or lower profitability. This risk-return trade-off is the key aspect of financial management. Furthermore, a financial director's propensity to take risks can lead to less or more conservative financial decisions.

This study firstly provides theoretical issues on financial management and the results of previous research, while the second part is empirical, showing the methodology and results of the authors' research. Apart from CFO risk attitude, the book also examines CFO power. The book highlights the importance of the position of financial managers in companies and demonstrates that financial decisions are the reflection of decision-makers' characteristics. Additionally, the book provides evidence of whether the COVID-19 crisis has increased or decreased the impact of CFO characteristics on financial decision-making and firm performance.

The book will attract the attention of researchers and students of corporate finance and accounting and also contains many valuable tips and insights for practitioners.

Elżbieta Bukalska is an Associate Professor in the Department of Corporate Finance and Accounting, Maria Curie-Sklodowska University, Lublin, Poland.

Anna Wawryszuk-Misztal is an Assistant Professor in the Department of Corporate Finance and Accounting, Maria Curie-Sklodowska University, Lublin, Poland.

Tomasz Sosnowski is an Assistant Professor at the Faculty of Economics and Sociology at the University of Lodz, Poland.

Routledge Focus on Economics and Finance

The fields of economics are constantly expanding and evolving. This growth presents challenges for readers trying to keep up with the latest important insights. Routledge Focus on Economics and Finance presents short books on the latest big topics, linking in with the most cutting-edge economics research.

Individually, each title in the series provides coverage of a key academic topic, whilst collectively the series forms a comprehensive collection across the whole spectrum of economics.

Well-being and Growth in Advanced Economies
The Need to Prioritise Human Development
Maurizio Pugno

The Economics of ObamaCare
Łukasz Jasiński

Monetary Policy and Inflation
Quantity Theory of Money
Mateusz Machaj

Customer Data Sharing Frameworks
Twelve Lessons for the World
Anton Didenko, Natalia Jevglevskaja and Ross P. Buckley

Crowdfunding European Business
Antonella Francesca Cicchiello

The Chief Financial Officer and Corporate Performance
Finance, Governance and Risk
Elżbieta Bukalska, Anna Wawryszuk-Misztal and Tomasz Sosnowski

For more information about this series, please visit: www.routledge.com/Routledge-Focus-on-Economics-and-Finance/book-series/RFEF

The Chief Financial Officer and Corporate Performance

Finance, Governance and Risk

Elżbieta Bukalska,
Anna Wawryszuk-Misztal
and Tomasz Sosnowski

Routledge
Taylor & Francis Group

LONDON AND NEW YORK

First published 2024
by Routledge
4 Park Square, Milton Park, Abingdon, Oxon OX14 4RN

and by Routledge
605 Third Avenue, New York, NY 10158

Routledge is an imprint of the Taylor & Francis Group, an informa business

© 2024 Elżbieta Bukalska, Anna Wawryszuk-Misztal and Tomasz Sosnowski

The right of Elżbieta Bukalska, Anna Wawryszuk-Misztal and Tomasz Sosnowski to be identified as authors of this work has been asserted in accordance with sections 77 and 78 of the Copyright, Designs and Patents Act 1988.

British Library Cataloguing-in-Publication Data
A catalogue record for this book is available from the British Library

Library of Congress Cataloging-in-Publication Data
Names: Bukalska, Elżbieta, author. | Wawryszuk-Misztal, Anna, author. |
Sosnowski, Tomasz (College teacher), author.
Title: The chief financial officer and corporate performance : finance, governance and risk / Elżbieta Bukalska, Anna Wawryszuk-Misztal and Tomasz Sosnowski.
Description: Abingdon, Oxon ; New York, NY : Routledge, 2024. |
Series: Routledge focus on economics and finance |
Includes bibliographical references and index.
Identifiers: LCCN 2023056844 (print) | LCCN 2023056845 (ebook) |
ISBN 9781032752808 (hardback) | ISBN 9781032752822 (paperback) |
ISBN 9781003473190 (ebook)
Subjects: LCSH: Business enterprises--Finance. | Corporations--Finance. |
Chief financial officers.
Classification: LCC HG4026 .B84 2024 (print) |
LCC HG4026 (ebook) | DDC 658.15--dc23/eng/20240109
LC record available at https://lccn.loc.gov/2023056844
LC ebook record available at https://lccn.loc.gov/2023056845

ISBN: 978-1-032-75280-8 (hbk)
ISBN: 978-1-032-75282-2 (pbk)
ISBN: 978-1-003-47319-0 (ebk)

DOI: 10.4324/9781003473190

Typeset in Times New Roman
by KnowledgeWorks Global Ltd.

Contents

Figures

Tables

Introduction

Company activity consists of real and financial aspects. The financial sphere (resources and processes) enhances the real sphere (resources and processes). Financial management should create a current and future environment for effective real activity allowing to strengthen the company's market position. But each real decision and activity has financial results.

Financial management covers several issues (investment and financing decisions, net working capital management) and requires a lot of rules (e.g. referring to the financial statement, time value of money, relations between risk and rate of return, cost of capital). Because financial management is a set of complex activities, it should be performed by a professional – financial manager/financial director/chief financial officer. The person in charge should have sufficient knowledge of corporate finance and the financial market (institutions and instruments). But he is expected not only to monitor the financial results of the decisions but also to be actively involved in the company's running. The scope of duties is quite wide and requires both knowledge and skills to operate in a more demanding environment.

Since 80-ies of the XX century, along with the changes in the product market and capital market, it is more common to promote a financial manager to the rank of the chief (often second to the chief executive officer). Promoting the finance manager to its strategic role leads to promoting the finance manager to the level of chief and member of the board of directors. Additionally, the financial director drew a lot of attention in academic research.

The role of the CFOs was reduced due to the financial scandals, misstatement affairs, and financial crisis at the beginning of the XX century. But recent crises (the COVID-19 crisis, Ukraine-Russia war), climate negative changes, energy transformation, and sustainable development challenge the current company running. These changes create new requirements for finance function, obtaining capital, and the role of CFOs. Additionally, the development of the financial markets, globalization, and internationalization make the finance function more difficult. We believe that the world is turning into a stagnation age accompanied by inflation and increasingly more difficult operating environment. All of these require specific skills and competencies from financial managers.

DOI: 10.4324/9781003473190-1

Many theoretical conceptions try to explain how demographic characteristics of managers (e.g. gender, educational backgrounds) affect organizational behaviour and financial performance. These relationships are usually explained by upper echelons theory, resource dependence theory, human capital theory, social capital theory, or agency theory.

Since it was proved that financial policy depends on the personal attitude towards risk or the level of overconfidence of executives, it is widely accepted that observable demographic characteristics might be used as proxies. This approach is applied by many researchers who analyse the relationship between demographic dimensions of executives (CEO, CFO) and financial decisions such as capital structure, cash holdings, investments etc. However, the results provided by the literature are mixed.

Therefore we are going to find the relationship between the CFOs' characteristics and financial decisions (cash holdings, capital structure), and then analyse if the CFOs' individual characteristics are associated with the firm's financial performance. Our research uses both: indirect (demographic characteristics, overconfidence) and direct measures. Apart from CFO risk attitude (coming from direct and indirect features), we include in our research CFO power. Despite the CFOs' risky attitude (due to personal characteristics or overconfidence), the actual CFO impact might be limited to traditional functions (due to low CFO power).

To identify the psychological dimensions of CFOs (i.e. the level of risk aversion) we built the survey questionnaire. We were able to collect 155 survey responses from CFOs of Polish companies. Based on the data collected, we developed several indexes describing in a synthetic way the CFO's power and the CFO's risk attitude. We also developed four clusters of CFOs depending on their demographic characteristics. Later, we aimed to find whether the demographic characteristics, risk attitude, and CFO power affect the financial decisions (capital structure, cash holdings) and firm performance.

The book consists of six chapters. The first chapter includes a general description of corporate finance, financial management, and the role of financial managers. This chapter provides the first evidence of the increasing role of the financial manager, more often appointed to the board of directors.

The second chapter provides a literature review of the CFO's demographic characteristics. This chapter presents also the research findings on the relationship between CFO's demographic characteristics, financial decisions, and firm performance.

The third chapter provides the methodological background of our research. We describe our research model and formulate research hypotheses. We also present our research tool – the survey – with a thorough description of the questions asked. We finish this chapter with sample characteristics – the distribution of answers within all researched areas.

The fourth chapter shows how chosen demographic characteristics affect the perceived role and impact of financial directors. We developed four clusters of CFOs grouped according to their age, gender, education, and professional experience. Additionally, we develop four indexes describing CFOs' risk attitude and their power.

In the fifth chapter, we connect CFOs' characteristics with corporate finance, especially financial decisions (capital structure, cash holdings) and firm performance (profitability). To find this relationship, we employed ANOVA (analysis of variance) F-test for equality of means and median chi-square test, and OLS regression analysis.

The last, sixth chapter provides a discussion of the research results with the previous findings on the role of CFOs from different countries. We present several similarities but also differences between our results and previous results.

We believe that our research might be interesting for practitioners, academics, and students. We present a literature review on the CFO role and CFO demographic characteristics. We also present the previous research findings on the impact of CFO on financial decisions and firm performance. Additionally, we conduct our own research and present our results which partially confirm previous research. We believe that this is the first research in Poland on the role of CFOs.

1 The role of the financial director in financial management

1.1 The theory of financial management

1.1.1 The concept of financial management

Company activity leads to the production of goods and services. This is a result of introducing the factors of production into a specific manufacturing process. This is done in order to meet the customers' needs and in the result to earn sales revenue and income and increase the equity value (the value of capital invested by shareholders).

The company consists of two layers: resources and processes (Karpuś, 2006, p. 13; Brealey et al., 2012). Resources might be tangible or intangible, real or financial. Resources are the base for the company's activity as they are used in the processes. Processes are series of logically related activities or tasks (such as provision, production, or sales) performed together to produce a set of results. Within the processes, there are flows of different resources: real and financial (Kolb and Rodriguez, 1992; Karpuś, 2006, p. 13; Brealey et al., 2012). Real processes are connected with the flow of real goods (such as material, services, and goods, e.g.: material receipt to storage, and product transfer to customers). Financial processes are connected with the flow of money, e.g.: paying for raw materials, collecting money from customers, paying dividends, and getting loans.

All the real resources and processes need financial support. And financial sphere (resources and processes) enhances the real sphere (resources and processes). The real and financial spheres are mutually dependent (Karpuś, 2006, p. 13; Brealey et al., 2012). The financial activity of the company supports the real activity of the company. Financial management should create a current and future environment for effective real activity allowing to strengthen the market position. But each real decision and activity has financial results. Real activities result in the level and the structure of assets. The assets can work out cash flow with the specific level of risk, and these cash flows will affect current and future owners' and creditors' interests (Karpuś, 2006, p. 13; Brealey et al., 2012).

DOI: 10.4324/9781003473190-2

Thus, corporate finance might be defined as the flows of funds in the financial sphere as the result of real sphere activities and to support activities in the real sphere. Financial management is the management of the funds flows – funds gaining and allocating (among real sphere activities in the company) (Kolb and Rodriguez, 1992; Brealey et al., 2012).

1.1.2 Market and financial management

The company runs its activities with a strong connection with the market. One can find:

* goods and services market;
* factors of production market (input market).

Both the real sphere and financial sphere are connected with the goods and services market and the input (factors of production) market (Karpuś, 2006, p. 23; Brealey et al., 2012). The company sells its goods and services on the goods and services market. In turn, customers pay for the goods bought. So, the real goods come from the company to the market, and cash flows from the market to the company.

The company buys raw materials, energy, and water supplies on the market for factors of production. In turn, the company pays for these purchases. So, the real goods come from the market to the company, and cash flows from the company to the market.

A specific but important element of factors of production market is a financial market where a company can acquire capital. Capital is one, apart from natural resources and work, of the factors of production, and a company can go to the financial market and obtain capital.

The financial market is a set of conditions in which some market participants can save excess cash (supply of capital, lenders, investors) and some can use the accumulated cash (demand for capital, borrowers, and issuers) (Pilbeam, 2010; Brealey et al., 2012). There are a lot of financial institutions (e.g. banks, stock exchange) and financial instruments (e.g. bonds and shares) that make the flow of capital between the supply and demand side on the financial market (Copeland et al., 2005).

There are different classifications and types of financial market. The most known is that one dividing the financial market into money market and capital market. The money market deals with short-term instruments (e.g. commercial papers), while the capital market deals with long-term instruments (e.g. shares and bonds). The capital market consists of the equity market and debt market. An equity market is a market where ownership of securities issued and subscribed is known as equity market. An example of an equity market for shares is the New York Stock Exchange (NYSE) and the Warsaw Stock

Exchange (WSE). Debt market is a market where funds are borrowed and lent is known as debt market. Arrangements are made in such a way that the borrowers agree to pay the lender the original amount of the loan plus some specified amount of interest. An example of a debt market is Catalyst.

The financial market might be primary and secondary. Newly issued securities are bought or sold in the primary market (e.g. Initial Public Offering). The transactions in the primary market are done between issuers and investors. The secondary market allows investors to buy and sell already existing securities. The transactions in the secondary market are done between investors (Copeland et al., 2005).

The company might be a lender of capital. When companies have surplus cash that is not needed for a short period of time, they may seek to make money from their cash surplus by lending it via short-term markets (money market) or long-term investment via long-term market (capital market). Alternatively, such companies may decide to return the cash surplus to their shareholders (e.g. via a share repurchase or dividend payment). However, companies usually borrow money to enhance short-term or long-term growth.

The financial market is important for the whole economy as it has some specific functions (e.g. allocation and valuation). But also the financial market is important for the company. The financial market supports the company in the following ways (Karpuś, 2006, p. 24; Brealey et al., 2012):

• arranging the payment system – using credit cards or online bank accounts makes the payment for goods' buying and selling faster, easier, and cheaper;
• maintaining financial liquidity – buying or selling short-term commercial papers allows management of cash deficit or surplus with quite low costs;
• company growing – by issuing shares or bonds company can acquire capital and invest it in profitable investment projects that strengthen the company's market position;
• accessing to the information on the cost of capital – the result of the game of capital supply and demand is interest rate (cost of capital) which shows the lowest level for investment projects rate of return.

The connections with markets (input, financial, goods) create a specific financial model of business. The financial model of business is presented in Figure 1.1.

The company acquires capital in the financial market by issuing equity or debt instruments. The investors by buying financial instruments invest in the company and expect the rate of return. Then the collected capital is invested by the company in investment projects. The company buys machinery and inventory, runs operating activity, and sells products in the goods and service market. By running a business, the company creates a portfolio of business projects. And the company expects a rate of return on their investment. The

Funds collection (debt and equity)

Investing collected funds in fixed and current assets

Buying machinery, buying materials, workers hiring

Financial market

Company

Real goods market

Income distribution (interests and dividends)

Income generating from assets

Goods and services selling

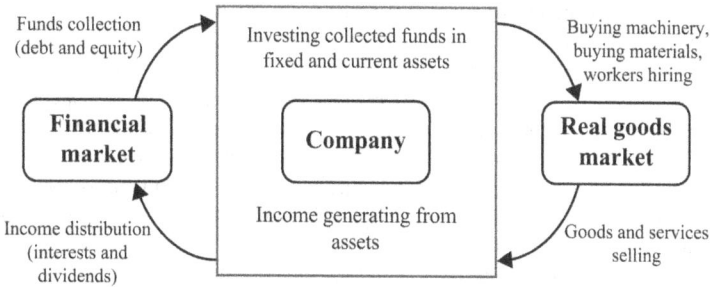

Figure 1.1 Financial model of business

difference between sales revenues and costs shows the profit of the company. Part of the profit is distributed among the investors (among owners and creditors according to their expectations) and the rest of the profit is reserved for the next investment projects in the company (reinvested, reserve capital).

1.1.3 The goals of financial management

The goal of financial management should be subordinated to the main goal of the company. There are different wordings of the company goal: to survive, to avoid financial distress, to beat the competition, to maximize sales or market share, to minimize costs, and to maintain steady earnings growth. Some people think that the appropriate goal can be stated as the maximization of net profit. Others think that the appropriate goal can be stated as the maximization of the current value per share of the existing stock/maximization of the market value of the owners' equity (Ross et al., 1993; Copeland et al., 2005).

On the one hand, net profit turns out to be the financial item that is easily misreported. The ENRON case proves that there are a lot of possibilities to show a higher value of net profit than it really is (accounting manipulations: recording the revenue before dispatching the goods). The company might take some actions that will increase net profit in the short-term but will have negative long-term results (the company might increase the net profit by decreasing R&D expenses) (Latham and Braun, 2010).

On the other hand, market value is the result of the investors' behaviour (demand and supply side). Investors' behaviour depends on their psychological and cognitive mental process (some fallacies and biases, moods and emotions). Investors might follow the behaviours of other investors (herd behaviour) (Mobarek et al., 2014). Additionally, investors might be misled by inappropriate managers' behaviour. The managers might take only these actions that will gain positive investors' response (increase in market share prices) no matter whether it is good for the company's long-term running (e.g. paying generous dividends) (Kothari et al., 2016). This makes that market value unrelated to the fundamental (intrinsic) value of the company.

Generally, the company goal can be stated as the following: creating value for customers by meeting the expectations of creditors and other stakeholders (employees, cooperating companies) and increasing the equity value. This attitude is in line with stewardship (stakeholder) theory (Jensen, 2010). But when the aim is determined, the agency approach might be also applied. Agency theory assumes that the company is managed in favour of one group only – shareholders (Glinkowska and Kaczmarek, 2015).

Knowing why the company is in business, several functional goals (e.g. production goals and sales targets) were identified. They should be coherent and supportive of the general goal of the company. One of the company's functions is the financial one. Financial management should financially support the general strategy, and at the same time ensuring the financial health of the company and allowing the company to grow in the long term.

1.1.4 The scope of financial decisions

There are three main aspects of financial decisions (Ross et al., 1993, pp., 6–8; Brealey et al., 2012):

- investment decisions – connected with long-term growth and fixed assets (machinery, buildings, and business) purchase;
- financing decisions – connected with raising capital both debt and equity and the company's activity on the financial market;
- net working capital management – connected with everyday business and inventory, receivables, cash, and liabilities management.

The investment decisions should provide the growth of the company and involve only profitable projects ensuring the improvement of market position. Investment in fixed assets gives ground for the business to run. All the investment projects should be profitable after meeting positive Net Present Value requirements. There are different ways of the company growth – by organic growth or through mergers and acquisitions. The value and structure of newly bought fixed assets should match the strategy – if the general strategy assumes active and fast growth, then the value of investment projects is bigger. Apart from new investment projects, the company should also think in terms of increasing the efficiency of already bought fixed assets. If the company has assets that do not generate expected profits, it should get rid of them. The fixed assets are the source of income generating with a specific operating (business) risk. The effectiveness of using machinery determines the company's profitability.

The financing decisions referring to raising funds should provide support for investment decisions. The value of capital gained should suit the value of capital expenditure in an investment project (financial engineering). The company should decide what is the source of capital – issuing shares or bonds, gaining bank loans, or retaining net profit (paying dividends). Gaining capital requires co-operating with the financial market and its institutions. Each source of capital differs in terms of the procedure of acquiring the capital, and necessary paper that should be produced within the procedure, flexibility of using the money, time of collecting money, cost of capital, and impact on financial risk. Not only the value and the source of the capital is important but also the capital structure should be in the centre of the financing decisions. The capital structure decisions refer to the debt-equity relations. Some theories show that capital structure has an impact on the average cost of capital and company value (Modigliani and Miller theory without and with taxes, trade-off theory of optimal capital structure).

Net working capital is calculated as the difference between the current assets (e.g. accounts receivable, inventories, and cash) and current liabilities. Net working capital management refers to the everyday business running and decisions on the level of inventory, receivables, cash, and operating liabilities. Net working capital management should be incorporated into investment and financing strategies. The inventory level and structure should match the fixed assets and operating activity depending on the industry the company belongs. The current assets (e.g. materials) enable to use the fixed assets (machinery) and in this way enhance the efficiency of fixed assets. The operating liabilities should match the financing and capital structure decisions. Net working capital elements affect also the financial liquidity level that reflects the safety of the business. There are a lot of benefits the company gets by possessing current assets, but they also entail costs (e.g. costs of inventory storage, recovery costs of receivables, and opportunity costs of cash). There are some methods of optimizing the level of net working capital elements (e.g. Baumol model, EOQ model, and Sartoris-Hill model).

These three aspects of financial decisions (investment, financing, and net working capital management) might be implemented in their conservative or aggressive version. Conservative or aggressive choice results in different levels of risk: conservative strategy is less risky, while aggressive strategy is more risky. However, there is a trade-off between risk and profitability (rate of return). Generally, there is a positive relation between risk and profitability: risky activities are more profitable.

These three aspects of financial decisions are mutually connected and should provide support for general strategy and fit for purpose. However, one should bear in mind that all company decisions and activities have financial implications. And before implementing any specific action the company should check what is the financial result of it and all planned activities. The company should also assess the impact of these activities on achieving the company goal but also on sustaining financial health (especially profitability and financial liquidity).

1.1.5   The specific issues affecting financial management

When managing corporate finance, one should consider several issues (Brealey et al., 2012):

- the relationship between owners and managers;
- financial statement and financial analysis;
- the relation between risk and rate of return;
- operating (business) risk and effects of financial leverage;
- cost of capital;
- time value of money.

If managers are to act in the interest of owners (maximize the market value of owners' equity) in some companies, there is a separation of ownership and management. Agency relations are the relations between stockholders (the principal) and managers (an agent). There is the possibility of conflicts of interest between the principal and the agent. Managers might have different goals than owners (Jensen and Meckling, 1976; Fama and Jensen, 1983; Ross et al., 1993). Managers might prefer buying another company in order to increase the size of the company or to demonstrate power or wealth instead of effectively using already possessed assets.

Agency costs refer to the costs of the conflict of interest. Indirect costs is a loss of opportunity. Direct costs have two types: one is a corporate expenditure that benefits management but costs stockholders (company car, empire building, and overinvestment). The second type is an expense that arises from the need to monitor management actions. Paying outside auditors to assess the accuracy of financial statements could be an example.

Existing research allows to identification of several types of agency tools that are to discipline managers and align their interest with shareholders' interest (Panda and Leepsa, 2017):

- blockholders, managerial ownership, executive remunerations, managerial labour market, and market for corporate control;
- appointing independent members to the supervisory board and board of directors;
- debt and dividend payment – debt and dividend payment decreases the internal funds and make the managers more cautious regarding making inefficient decisions that may hamper the profitability of the firm.

Due to the separation of ownership and control, the owners can follow the company activity through managers' decisions and course of action. The asymmetry of information on the company performance arises between outsider shareholder and insider managers. This asymmetry makes insider managers better informed and each of their decisions and actions is perceived as a signal of current and future firm situations (Myers and Majluf, 1984; Morellec and Schürhoff, 2011). There is an abundant number of research showing that announcing the decision to gain bank loan or to pay dividend out are strong signals that affect investors' behaviour (see Gupta and Aggarwal, 2018; Pauka and Żyła, 2018).

One way of diminishing the information asymmetry is to produce and publish financial statement (Graham et al., 2005). The financial statement presents in a unified way the financial results of company running. The financial statement consists of profit and loss statement (income statement), balance sheet, and cash flow statement. Financial statement is a good source of information for all outside stakeholders (e.g.: owners, co-operating companies, and financial institutions) to get a full picture of company performance. One might use financial analysis and financial ratios to deepen the knowledge on the company (Beaver et al., 2011). On the basis of the financial ratio, the company is able to predict the bankruptcy probability.

The financial ratios allow to assessment the profitability and financial liquidity. Some research shows that there is a trade-off between liquidity and profitability as profitability reflects growth opportunities and rate of return while liquidity reflects risk and business continuity (Eljelly, 2004). This trade-off assumes that the higher profitability (higher rate of return) is connected with lower liquidity (higher risk) and vice versa. The risk-return trade-off is quite well recognized and confirmed in many financial models (e.g.: CAPM model) (Fama and French, 2004).

Financial statements and financial ratios are useful in assessing operating (business) and financial risk. The business risk refers to the volatility of operating profit under the pressure of business environmental factors (such as demand). The financial risk refers to the volatility of net profit because of using debt (liabilities). Using debt companies can leverage their profits (positive effects of financial leverage) but also downsize their profits (negative effects of financial leverage). The direction of debt impact (positive or negative) depends on the level of operating profit and business risk – high operating profit and low business risk allow to achieve positive effects of financial leverage while low operating profits and high business risk lead to negative effects of financial leverage (Ghosh et al., 2000).

Another issue affecting financial management is the cost of capital. The cost of capital reflects the cost of the capital gained and served. In some cases, it is connected with cash flows (e.g. cost of bank loans) and in some cases, it is opportunity costs (e.g. cost of equity). There are several ways of assessing the cost of capital – e.g. Capital Assets Pricing Model (CAPM) (Levi and Welch, 2017). In the result, the company is able to calculate the cost of total capital by using the concept of weighted average (weighted average cost of capital, WACC). WACC should reflect the rate of return expected by investors with the risk of the company taken into account. WACC has several applications – might be used as the discount rate in capital budgeting decisions and discounting future expected cash flows (Copeland et al., 2005; Johnson and Qi, 2008; Berry et al., 2014).

Discounting future cash flow is connected with the time value of money. The time value of money concept assumes that money decreases its value with time. Future cash flows are less valuable than present cash flows. This concept is especially important when comparing future benefits with present investment e.g. in capital budgeting decisions (Drake and Fabozzi, 2009).

1.2   The role of the financial director

1.2.1   Financial director functions

Financial management is a set of complex activities and should be performed by a professional – financial manager/financial director/chief financial officer. The person in charge should have sufficient knowledge of corporate finance but also the financial market (institutions and instruments). But he is expected not only to monitor the financial results of the decisions but also to be actively involved in the company's running. Financial managers' job ensures the sustainability of the company (by e.g. raising funds) and their actions directly affect the efficiency of the business (by e.g. implementing profitable investment projects). The financial director is responsible for fundraising but also should have control over the use of funds to ensure the achieving the company goal.

As any business activity has its financial implications it is necessary for financial manager to understand the relations between different functions in the company (e.g. provision, production, marketing, and human resources) in achieving the company goal. This means that the financial director should cooperate with other company managers.

The basic functions of the financial director are the following (Karpuś, 2006, p. 13; Brealey et al., 2012):

- financial planning – knowing necessary assumptions (the company goal, company strategy, and important activities to take) the financial director is able to present all the data in financial terms (e.g. the value of sales revenue, operating costs, and profits);
- evaluation of the investment projects – assessing the value of capital expenditure and assessing whether planned capital expenditure provides positive Net Present Value and is worth of implementing; the financial director should assess the cash inflows from each investment project;
- estimating the funds needed – depending on the volume of the profitable projects the need for additional funds can be identified;
- raising funds – deciding on the capital structure and deciding on the funds' source of origin (issuing shares or bonds, getting bank loans, or using retained earnings); the financial director should be aware that any source of

funds is costly and is connected with cash outflows (such as principal and interest, dividends);

- cash management on a daily basis – deciding on the date of payment from customers and to suppliers but also on other aspects of terms of payment (building relations with suppliers and customers), cash is required for many purposes like paying the electricity and water bills, paying to creditors, purchasing raw materials, paying wages and salaries, but also keep some cash reserves for unexpected expenditure or financing the growth of the company;
- financial controlling – exercising control over each decision having financial implications; the financial director should not only plan, procure, and utilize funds but also control the whole financial sphere of business running;
- presenting the financial results – entering financial information on the company activities into books and preparing the financial statements which are helpful for external users (e.g. investors existing and potential, creditors);
- activity on the financial market – providing investors with information on company activities but in general investor relations building; good relations with investors make additional funds acquiring easier. This is especially important for publicly listed companies but is important for private companies to keep good relations with banks, lease companies, and owners.

1.2.2 The relations between financial director and other managers

The decisions having financial implications are taken not only by the financial manager. The marketing manager makes a decision on the marketing plan or product sales price – which affects the value of sales revenue and marketing expenditure. The production manager makes a decision about what raw materials are necessary, where to buy them, and who is the best supplier of high-quality raw materials – which affect the cost expenditure but also affect the quality of the company product and the value of sales revenue.

All the decisions having financial implications, no matter what it is its nature – marketing or production or another, should be taken in cooperation with the financial director but also considering the main goal and strategy of the company. Each decision having financial implications should be also assessed in terms of its impact on the financial health of the company (i.e. profitability and financial liquidity).

The person in charge of financial management might have a different official position in the company (CFO or financial director) but this position should be equal to others involved in making decisions with financial implications. In smaller companies, the accounting manager is the person responsible both for financial management and for keeping records. But bigger companies usually hire the financial director who cooperates with accounting manager

Table 1.1 Differences in attitude towards financial decisions presented by financial director and accounting manager

Financial director	Accounting manager
Responsible for translating the company activities into financial dimension before taking a decision	Responsible for recording financial results of the company activities after the activity is accomplished
Co-operating with employees – other managers – when preparing the decisions to be taken	Co-operating with employees when collecting financial documents (e.g. invoices, stock documents, and payroll)
Co-operating with external stakeholders (banks and financial analysts) to create and develop strong bonds with financial market	Co-operating with external institution when providing financial statement (register court and tax office)
Subordinated to CEO/President of the company	Subordinated to financial director

in financial issues. But there are several differences between the attitude of the financial director and accounting manager towards financial decisions. Table 1.1 presents basic differences in attitude towards financial decisions presented by the financial director and accounting manager.

The scope of financial director duties depends on the size and stage of company life. In bigger and fast-growing companies, growing responsibilities and the increasing role of financial director leads sometimes to appointing the financial director to the board of directors. Sometimes, companies appoint a Chief Financial Officer as a full member of the board of directors. In this case, the CFO supervises the job of the financial manager who is responsible for everyday financial management.

1.2.3 The evolution of the role of the financial director in the company

For four decades after the Second World War (till 80ies of XX century) in countries of Western Europe and the United States the financial function was a back office function performed by treasurers or controllers, whose duties were confined to tasks like bookkeeping and preparing financial statements, and monitoring debt and capital structure (Zorn, 2004). Apart from overseeing reporting and preparing financial statements, the financial manager was also involved in creating the budget – typically well after production decisions had been made (Zorn, 2004; Whitley, 1986; Altman, 2002). Operational managers, from manufacturing to sales and marketing, dominated most decision-making processes in firms.

The changes started in the late 1970s and early 1980s. These years laid the foundation for the emergence of a new financial idea of control which, ultimately, would put the focus on "core competencies" and place the management of stock price at the very centre of corporate decision-making. During this period, the largest corporate organizations (especially in the US) underwent substantial reorganization. Along with the changes in the product market and capital market in the 1980s and 1990s, it is more common to promote financial managers to the rank of the chief (often second to the chief executive officer). This signalled a fundamental redistribution of managerial roles, with greater relevance of financial considerations built into the executive structure and decision-making process. Benefitting from their enhanced visibility and power, CFOs gained a critical say in key strategic and operational decisions, from evaluating business unit performance, inventing new ways to leverage capital, managing acquisition and divestitures, and fending off hostile takeover attempts, to serving as the company's primary ambassador to investors and financial analysts (Zorn, 2004; Sharma and Jones, 2010).

Promoting the finance manager to its strategic role leads to promoting the finance managers to the level of chief and member of the board of directors. The developments of the financial director's role are certainly reflective of increased capital market pressure to deliver satisfactory performance to shareholders. Equity and debt markets have offered sophisticated securities but also have become more challenging. The result is an increasing intensity of engagement between the CFO and the capital markets. The CFO came to manage relations with shareholders, market expectations, and the firm's stock price. CFOs held conference calls and reported updates about sales, costs, acquisitions, and divestitures much more frequently. Ultimately, the CFO's job thus came to involve not only public relations but also the development of accounting gimmicks that would enable firms to meet investors' expectations (Altman, 2002; Mellon et al., 2012).

Additionally, a wave of mergers in the 1980s (especially in the United States) put a significant percentage of corporations at risk of being taken over. The CFO became critical in fending off hostile takeover attempts, in part, because the adjustment of financial figures for inflation was extended to internal reporting. Firms issued and received hostile takeover bids, merged into or acquired other firms, divested of unrelated business units, and implemented stock buy-back programmes. This provided CFOs with a powerful strategic tool with which they could help their bosses better identify poorly performing business units (Zorn, 2004).

The accounting scandals in the early 2000s revealed the actual role of CFOs in the late 1990s. A lot of research was carried out to find out the role of CFOs in manipulating financial reports. Dichev et al. (2013), report the results of a survey of 169 CFOs in which 91 percent report inside pressure as a motivation to manage earnings. Based on a survey of 141 public company CFOs, Fink (2002) states that 17 percent of CFOs report being pressured to misrepresent their results by their companies' CEOs during the past five years. CFOs become involved in accounting manipulations under pressure from CEOs, rather than instigating such manipulations for immediate personal financial gain. Feng et al. (2011), conclude that a contributing factor in accounting fraud is that CFOs succumb to pressure from their more powerful CEOs, suggesting a dynamic tension between the two positions. Financial managers act in consensus or CEOs exert a dominant influence on financial reporting (Aboody and Kasznik 2000; Efendi et al. 2007; Francis et al. 2008; Lin et al. 2014). Jiang et al. (2010), found that powerful CEOs are linked with more aggressive earnings management (Geiger and North 2006; Jiang et al. 2010). These studies provide strong evidence of the CEO's influence on the reporting system and the role of the CFO. Although CFOs oversee and manage information and reporting systems, they are also responsible to the CEO (Mian 2001). This gives CEOs power over CFOs (Friedman, 2014). A CEO has the power to replace a CFO who does not follow the CEO's preferences (Mian, 2001; Fee and Hadlock 2004). CFOs were and remain CEO's agents (Graham and Harvey 2001, p. 194). Traditionally, CFOs were considered to be financial stewards of their companies and their role has not changed, despite widespread belief.

However, there is some research proving that in some situations CFO can have power over the CEO. The reason might lie in the specific legal regulation (such as SOX), individual demographic characteristics (e.g. expertise and professional experience), or specific ownership structure (Caglio et al., 2018; Baker et al., 2019).

One of the model approaches assumes that the role of the CFO is really four jobs in one. It requires calling these distinct roles the "four faces" of the CFO: Steward, Operator, Strategist, and Catalyst (Deloitte, 2007; Carson, 2012). These four roles are complementary, not exclusive, with a progression in the roles from being a Steward to a Strategist, from an Operator to a Catalyst. These varied roles make a CFO's job quite complex.

The Steward role entails keeping the books accurate as well as protecting and preserving the assets of the organization. A good Steward ensures the day-to-day financial recordkeeping, maintaining high internal control standards, and effective budgeting, planning, and forecasting systems, documented financial policies, and procedures. Financial Stewards must focus on delivering effective compliance and control mechanisms to preserve organizational assets and minimize risk. Financial Stewards focus on the assessment and mitigation of risk and compliance against applicable regulatory or legal requirements while running effective financial and reporting mechanisms.

The Operator function helps ensure the prudent use of resources by standardizing, consolidating, and automating processes and systems to eliminate redundancy and develop shared services. CFOs have to operate an efficient and effective finance organization providing a variety of services to the business such as financial planning and analysis, treasury, tax, and other finance operations.

The Strategist's role influences the organization's overall direction by providing financial leadership in the organization. A Strategist is involved in strategy formation, provides a financial perspective on new initiatives, and is focused on helping to define the strategic future of the organization. He/she also advises senior management on risk management, business continuity, and resource allocation, and provides a cost-benefit analysis of business cases for new initiatives and projects. A Strategist should ensure the development and maintenance of medium to long-term financial and asset management planning for the organization.

A Catalyst is an agent for change in the whole organization, and seeks out opportunities to achieve increased efficiency and effectiveness in service delivery. A Catalyst will install a financial mindset across the organization. Finance Catalysts focus on the disciplined execution of strategy throughout their organization and help to drive an attitude of delivering business value. A Catalyst gains business support to identify, evaluate, and execute strategies successfully by partnering with senior management and driving processes to define optimal targets and measure performance.

These four roles reflect two dimensions of the analysis:

- the relation with the CEO: as a business partner playing an important role in strategy formulation (Strategist) or as a subordinate playing a role in strategy execution (Steward);
- the relation to other business units: as an agent of change throughout the whole organization (Catalyst) or as a financial officer he/she focuses only on the financial function of the organization and on the relations with his/ her subordinates in the financial department (Operator).

***

Financial management is connected with financial resources and processes. Financial resources refer to cash but also each resource that its value might be presented in money. Financial management needs professional knowledge as the company's finance are connected to the real goods market and financial market. There are different financial institutions and financial instruments. There are also some basic issues, e.g.: financial statements, relations between risk and rate of return, relations between managers and owners, and cost of capital.

The scope of financial management includes capital collecting and capital allocating decisions. However, these decisions should be aligned with the general aim and strategy of the company. The decomposition of the financial manager functions leads to the identification of several activities such as financial planning, capital budgeting, raising funds, cash management, financial controlling, and financial statement preparation.

When financial management, the director is supposed to cooperate with internal and external stakeholders. For a long time, the financial director was supported by other directors, but recently its role and power have increased.

2 The financial director characteristics and financial decisions

2.1 Theory on the role of CFO characteristics in management decisions

A firm's financial performance is the result of financial decisions. According to many financial theories, the key to financial decisions is the risk-return trade-off. Since the corporate financial policy is shaped by executives, the literature shows that personal attitude towards risk and the overconfidence of decision-makers might be used as predictors of financial decisions and thus financial performance (Chava and Purnanandam, 2010; Graham et al., 2013; Sah et al., 2022). This indicates that managerial risk attitude and overconfidence play important roles in the decision-making process.

Risk attitude is defined as a state of mind about uncertainties that might positively or negatively affect the aims (Hillson and Murray-Webster, 2007 p. 6). In economics, it is expected that decision-maker's attitude towards risk results in riskier or more conservative financial decisions (König, 2021).

Risk attitude is a psychological dimension that affects executives' financial decisions. Attitude towards the risk of individuals is a non-observable (latent) psychological dimension and it is difficult to measure (see König, 2021). On the one hand, it is commonly accepted that demographic characteristics such as gender, age, and experience might reflect the non-observable values, cognitive base, and especially personal attitude towards risk. There is much research showing that risk aversion varies due to age, gender, and nationality (Harrison et al., 2007; Dohmen et al., 2017; Falk et al., 2018). Thus, they might be used as indirect measures of unobservable psychological dimensions of executives. However, the literature on financial decisions provides mixed evidence on the role of demographic dimensions of executives for financial decisions on capital structure, cash holdings, and investment (see Schopohl et al., 2021).

Also, overconfidence is quite often used as the proxy for risk attitude (Graham et al., 2013; Wrońska-Bukalska, 2016; Bukalska, 2020). Overconfidence is the conviction of a manager on having better knowledge and abilities than others, which refrains them from getting new information and from

DOI: 10.4324/9781003473190-3

listening to experts (Bukalska, 2020). The overconfident manager is inclined to overvalue his/her abilities and capabilities (Brown and Sarma, 2007) and optimism about the future. Since company overinvestment is perceived as a result of managerial overconfidence, many researchers identify the overconfidence of decision-makers with the propensity to take risk (Huang and Kisgen; 2013; Liu et al., 2022). It happens because, the overestimation of future earnings and underestimation of future losses is the feature of an overconfident manager (Larwood and Whittaker, 1977; Puri and Robinson, 2007). On the other hand, the literature regarding behavioural finance provides direct measures of managers' risk attitudes (Barsky et al., 1997). However, applying these methodologies requires the usage of the survey-based approach.

Many theoretical conceptions try to explain how demographic characteristics of managers (e.g. gender and educational backgrounds) affect organizational behaviour and financial performance. These relationships are usually explained by upper echelons theory, resource dependence theory, human capital theory, social capital theory, or agency theory.

The upper echelons theory of Hambrick and Mason (1984) states that managerial background characteristics partially influence the strategic choices and performance levels (p. 193). Thus, demographic characteristics of top managers (especially CEOs and CFOs) are important for outcomes of the company (Velte, 2020). According to the upper echelons theory, strategic choices of the company and its outcomes are reflections of the cognitive base and values of top managers, which, in turn, affect perception and interpretations of the strategic situations. Since these psychological dimensions are difficult to observe and measure, they can be replaced by observable demographic characteristics of top managers such as age, career experience, and education (Carpenter et al., 2004). It leads to the conclusion that managerial backgrounds allow one to predict the future behaviour of the organization.

The researchers analysing the relationship between board composition and organizational behaviour usually reveal to resource dependence theory (RDT) of Pfeffer and Salancik (1978). It states that an organization depends on the provision of unique resources, thus the company has to create inter-organization arrangements of various kinds to cope with interdependencies, and to get autonomy and legitimacy (Drees and Heugens, 2013). According to RDT, the special role is performed by top managers who provide to organization advice and counsel, and facilitate to gain the unique resources from the external environment (Pfeffer and Salancik, 1978). To perform these tasks effectively, the top managers should have relevant skills, competency, and experience, i.e. provide the relevant social and human capital to the organization. This statement emphasizes the linkage between the resource dependence theory and other theoretical concepts, i.e. human capital theory and social capital theory.

The concept of human capital was introduced to literature by Gary Becker in the sixties of the XX century (Weiss, 2015). Human capital is defined as the set of a person's productive skills that might be used to provide profits on the labour market and to increase a household's consumption possibilities (Weiss, 2015). Individuals can invest in their human capital and then utilize it in the work or household, but they can not buy or sell it on the market (Weiss, 2015). Schooling and learning on the job are the two types of investments in human capital over the life cycle. Human capital investments are the source of differences in wages among individuals of different ages, education, and experience. Given this, every individual brings to the organization unique skills and qualifications that are the result of their previous education and occupation (Hillman et al., 2002).

According to resource dependence theory, both human and social capital are provided to organizations by their directors. While the value of human capital depends on an individual's education, skills, and occupation, the value of social capital is created by the relationship between an individual or group and others (Portes, 1998). Social capital is the result of interpersonal linkages between directors and other people from inside and outside the firm (Kim and Cannella, 2008). They distinguish internal social capital, i.e. ties and relations with other people in the organization, and external social capital, i.e. ties and relations with external investors, customers, suppliers, legal authorities, and politicians (Kim and Cannella, 2008). The membership of board directors in social networks or social structures increases the value of social capital. Internal and external networks of board directors influence the strategy setting (Haynes and Hillman, 2010) which makes social capital an important issue.

Analysing the role of the CFO in financial decisions, agency, and stewardship theory should be mentioned. The work of Hiebl (2015) investigates different attitudes of CFOs that are associated with these theories. The separation of ownership and management contributes to the self-serving behaviour of managers, which is called "agency behaviour" (Le Breton-Miller et al., 2011). The agency-oriented managers are likely to place their private interests ahead of shareholders' goals. There are some examples of self-serving behaviour of CFOs, i.e. excessive compensation and involvement in low-return takeovers (Jensen and Meckling, 1976; Jensen, 1986; Eisenhardt, 1989; Shleifer and Vishny, 1997). The agency theory provides the tools that might align the interests of managers and owners, among which the most important are monitoring and incentive payments (Jensen and Meckling, 1976; Davis et al., 1997). Contrary to agency theory, the steward theory attitude is based on the assumption that managers subjugate their interests to increase the welfare of the owners. The steward-oriented managers can align their aims and long-term shareholders' goals (Hernandez, 2012).

From the theoretical perspective managers can behave as agents or stewards. Thus, the individual characteristics of managers are supposed to be important in explaining their attitude towards shareholders' aims. Following this, financial decisions, that contribute to realizing shareholders' aims, are affected by the individual characteristics of managers.

2.2 Demographic characteristics of executives and financial decisions

Since the financial policy depends on the personal attitude towards risk or the level of overconfidence of executives (Chava and Purnanandam, 2010), it is widely accepted that observable demographic characteristics might be used as the proxies of these psychological dimensions. This approach is applied by many researchers who analyse the relationship between demographic dimensions of executives (CEO and CFO) and financial decisions such as capital structure, cash holdings, investments, etc. However, the results provided by the literature are mixed.

2.2.1 *Gender of executives and financial decisions*

Academics analysing the differences between female and male directors appeal to the literature on psychology, which points to some gender behavioural differences such as attitude towards risk or overconfidence (Ho et al., 2015). The psychological research documents that female directors are more conservative, risk-averse, and less overconfident in comparison to their male counterparts (e.g., Byrnes et al., 1999; Croson and Gneezy 2009; Ho et al., 2015). Companies run by female directors choose strategies that reduce the company's risk and allow them to avoid losses. Therefore, more conservative financial decisions are expected in such companies. For example, Huang and Kisgen (2013) compared the largest US companies run by female and male directors and documented that female directors tend to make risk-averse decisions which leads to lower growth and a smaller number of acquisitions. Also, the research for Chinese companies provides evidence that female CFOs are more conservative than their male counterparts as regards financial policy (Han et al., 2020). This investigation reveals that in a high-growth industry female CFOs refrain from using external financing. Liu et al. (2022) report that female directors are more prone to reduce firm-level overinvestment which is in line with agency theory and confirms the risk-aversion attitude of female directors.

2.2.1.1 *Gender of executives and capital structure decisions*

Capital structure decisions which are the centre of financial decisions are associated with the leverage of the company. Many theoretical conceptions explain how the company makes decisions on capital structure: the trade-off theory, the agency theory, the pecking order theory, market timing theory (Harris and Raviv, 1991; Baker and Wurgler, 2002). The academics investigating the association between capital structure decisions and managerial characteristics usually apply the arguments provided by trade-off theory. This theory states that higher leverage, on the one hand, increases the risk of financial distress and insolvency, (Molina, 2005; Faccio et al., 2016) but on the other, it may lead to higher profitability. And conversely, lower leverage decreases the financial risk but might reduce the profitability. The literature shows that these trade-off decisions might be affected by the personal characteristics of the decision-maker, i.e. attitude towards risk. Therefore, one should expect that women's aversion towards risk might result in lower leverage or lower propensity to issue debt in companies managed by female directors.

The association between women's presence on boards and capital structure decisions has not been extensively studied so far (Zaid et al., 2020); however, negative relationship between the presence of women directors and the level of debt has been confirmed by some researchers. The investigation by Huang and Kisgen (2013) including US public companies reveals that companies with female executives less frequently issued debt in comparison with those run by male executives. Also, the research of Harris (2014) for US public companies confirms the negative association between the presence of women on board and the ratio of total debt to total assets. Since the investigation of Harris (2014) includes only companies with boards composed of at least 25% women directors those companies, it also gives support for critical mass theory, which states that the role of female directors might be marginalized if their number is smaller than the critical mass (Harris, 2014). This result confirms the risk aversion attitude of women directors. Similar results are reported for Spain's agricultural cooperatives (Hernández-Nicolás et al., 2019). Also, Faccio et al. (2016) report that female CEOs are associated with a lower willingness to use debt by companies from 18 countries. Schopohl et al. (2021) who examined the link between women's presence among executives and the level of leverage of UK public companies report that companies with female CFOs are less prone to use debt than firms with men in CFO positions. However, the negative association between female CFOs and leverage is observed under some conditions., i.e. the firm is run by not powerful CEO, the composition of the board is diversified, and the women taking the CFO position is externally appointed (Schopohl et al., 2021).

Nevertheless, some researchers report a higher propensity of female directors to increase indebtedness. Rossi et al. (2018) who examined Italian non-financial public companies from 2005 to 2013 report that greater women's representation on the board increases the usage of debt by companies. It means that female directors are better agency cost monitors in comparison with their male counterparts. This result is in line with the arguments provided by agency theory. However, the role of female directors in Italian companies depends on their position on the board. A company has a lower level of debt, when on the board there is a woman who has family connections with the company's owners (Rossi et al., 2018).

2.2.1.2 Gender of executives and cash holdings decisions

Decisions on cash holdings affect the financial liquidity of the company. There are three main theoretical models explaining which factors affect the amount of cash held by companies: the trade-off model, the pecking order theory (Myers, 1984), and the free cash flow hypothesis of Jensen (1986). According to the trade-off model, the company targets the optimal level of cash when the marginal benefit and marginal cost of holding cash. Holding cash decreases the likelihood of financial distress and bankruptcy, it allows to continue the investment policy when external financing is limited and costly (Ferreira and Vilela, 2004). These benefits are explained by precautionary motives for holding cash, which are perceived as a buffer protecting the company against bankruptcy. However, the cash reserves create an opportunity cost as the rate of return on liquid assets is low. Thus, the company has to compare the benefits and costs of holding cash and choose a decision based on the trade-off base.

Contrary to the trade-off model, the pecking order theory (Myers, 1984) states that the company does not set the optimal level of cash reserves. The level of liquid assets depends on investment needs and retained earnings. The cash is accumulated if operational cash flow is higher than the investment needs and debt repayments. However, the cash reserves are reduced if the retained earnings are too low to finance investment (Ferreira and Vilela, 2004).

According to the free cash flow hypothesis of Jensen (1986), the managers aim to increase the liquid assets as it allows them to make investment decisions regardless of the availability of external financing. On the one hand, this situation allows to maintain the asymmetry of information, i.e. the managers do not have to provide information about the future projects. On the other hand, as the investment projects are not evaluated by external investors, the risk of making decisions that might decrease shareholder's wealth is high. Therefore, the large cash reserves increase the agency conflict between managers and shareholders.

Each of these theories provides a set of factors that might play an important role in determining the cash holdings decision. For example, taking the perspective of the trade-off model, the larger size of the company might hurt cash holdings, but the pecking order theory or free cash flow hypothesis assumes a positive impact (Ferreira and Vilela, 2004).

The studies on cash holdings determinants pay attention to the firm-specific characteristics as predictors of liquidity policy. One of these characteristics is firms' financial constraints. Based on the precautionary motive for holding cash, the researchers argue that high cash resources allow the company to avoid financial distress if access to external financing is limited or costly. Conversely, financially less-constrained companies are more likely to reduce cash reserves as they can easily gain capital from financial markets. Opler et al.

(1999) document that the ability to gain external financing by company reduces the need to hold great cash reserves by US public companies. However, the smaller and riskier companies, with great growth opportunities, usually hold more cash than other firms (Opler et al., 1999). Also, the investigation of Han and Qiu (2007) provides evidence that financially constrained companies hold more cash due to precautionary motives. Apart from firm-level determinates of cash holdings, the literature points to the following groups of determinants: macroeconomic environment (Pinkowitz et al., 2013), institutions (Dudley and Zhang, 2016; Habib and Hasan, 2017), and industry characteristics (Haushalter et al., 2007). It is also reported that corporate governance factors, especially demographic characteristics of board members, might play an important role in liquidity decisions (see Harford et al., 2008).

The literature documents that usually the precautionary motives for holding cash and agency theory are used to explain the role of executives' characteristics (especially gender) in cash policy (Xu et al., 2019). Based on precautionary motives, one should perceive the cash reserves as a buffer against financial constrain and bankruptcy. It allows to implementation of business and investment policy if access to the external market is limited or costly. The role of precautionary motives for cash holdings decisions arises from the personal attitude towards risk of the decision-maker. This personal attitude depends on demographic characteristics such as gender, age, education, professional expertise, etc. Thus, the higher risk aversion of executives might result in higher cash reserves. For example, since female directors are inclined to avoid risky decisions to mitigate the risk of financial distress (Xu et al., 2019), higher cash reserves are expected in companies run by female directors.

However, the agency theory provides an opposite assumption on the directors' characteristics on the liquidity policy. According to agency theory, the influence of managers' behaviour is based on self-interest, thus they are inclined to accumulate cash to finance investment projects with negative NPV (Jensen and Meckling, 1976), which wastes the shareholders' wealth. Some researchers document that the liquid assets held by companies are higher in countries with poor protection of shareholders' rights (Dittmar et al., 2003). It means that the quality of corporate governance affects the cash holdings decision. Taking the microeconomic perspective, the level of cash holdings is affected by the behaviour of executives. The managers' tendency to hold excessive cash reserves is higher if they are less prone to ethical conduct. One should notice that the willingness to ethical behaviour is affected by demographic characteristics of executives. A large body of literature (see. Xu et al., 2019, p. 437) provides evidence of gender differences in ethical behaviour. For example, Isidro and Sobral (2015) provide evidence that women's presence on the board of the largest European companies has a positive impact on a firm's compliance with ethical and social principles. It is expected that the female executives would reduce managerial opportunism, to protect shareholders' interests and diminish agency conflict. Therefore, according to agency, theory one would predict that the companies run by female directors hold less liquid assets than firms conducted by male directors.

The existing research regarding the role of female directors in decisions regarding cash holdings provides mixed results. Zeng and Wang (2015) report a positive relationship between female CEOs and cash holdings for Chinese companies. Similar results were also achieved by Adhikari (2018) for companies included in the Compustat, CRSP, and Execucomp data sets and La Rocca et al. (2019) for companies from 18 countries, who provide evidence that companies with a greater number of female executives hold more cash. This investigation confirms the precautionary reasons for holding cash, not the agency theory. Also, the investigation of US companies covering the period from 1992 to 2013 gives support to the risk-averse attitude of female CEOs, which leads to less risky financial policies and higher cash reserves (Sah et al., 2022). The positive association between women's presence on management boards and cash holdings is also observed in Polish public companies (Wawryszuk-Misztal, 2021a). A similar association also exists in the case of supervisory boards, but this association is stronger if a female board member has family connections with the company's owners. Contradictory results were achieved by Atif et al. (2019) for US companies. They report that cash holdings are high if the percentage of female directors is lower. This investigation suggests that the arguments provided by agency theory are true. It means that female directors perform their monitoring role perfectly and contribute to reducing agency problems. Doan and Iskandar-Datta (2020) document that female CFOs reduce the cash reserves in companies with excessive cash, which results in higher dividends and agency conflict reduction. This investigation provides arguments for gender-ethics, not risk-aversion, hypothesis. However, other researchers, who analysed data from US-listed companies for the 2000–2017 period, report that the presence of women on board does not affect cash holdings (Tosuk et al., 2022).

The researchers also pay attention to the role of women on the corporate boards. The research of Cambrea et al. (2019) for Italian public companies reveals that larger cash holdings are observed in companies run by female CEOs. However, if women perform monitoring functions, they intend to reduce cash reserves to mitigate agency problems. The investigation of the sample of Chinese public companies (Xu et al., 2019) gives evidence that only the female CFO has a positive and significant impact on cash holdings, but there is no statistically significant association between female CEO and cash reserves.

The literature documents that financial constraints might have a moderating effect on the female executives' decisions on cash holdings. Xu et al. (2019) divided the research sample into two groups: financially constrained and unconstrained firms. A positive and significant association between cash holdings and female CFOs was observed among the sample of financially constrained companies, but this relationship was insignificant for unconstrained companies. This result confirms that female CFOs are conservative and tend to avoid the risk. Undoubtedly, this result gives support for the precautionary reasons for holding cash.

2.2.1.3   Gender of executives and working capital policy

Working capital management is one of the main financial decisions. Since it affects both a company's liquidity (i.e. risk) and profitability (i.e. return), the literature points to three policies of working capital: aggressive, conservative, and matching (or moderate) policy (Khan et al., 2022). The aggressive policy of working capital management assumes that a company aims at reducing current assets and increasing current liabilities, which finally results in decreasing the level of net working capital. This strategy allows to reduce the costs of financing and carrying costs but increases the risk of bankruptcy as the level of current assets might be insufficient to continue operating activity and meet required liabilities. Conversely, the conservative policy, which assumes that a company has to hold a high level of current assets and a low level of short-term liabilities allows it to reduce risk, but at the same time, it reduces the company's profitability. And finally, the issue of the matching policy is to balance both the level of current assets and current liabilities and thus the level of working capital is not too high and not too low. Under the matching policy, the company's profitability and risk of bankruptcy are at a moderate level.

The large strand of literature investigates the impact of working capital management decisions on a firm's efficiency (see Arnaldi et al., 2021; Bolek et al., 2021; Deari et al., 2022). The positive association between aggressive working capital practices and a firm's profitability or value is documented by many researchers (i.e. Deloof, 2003; García-Teruel and Martinez-Solano, 2007; Nguyen et al., 2020; Arnaldi et al., 2021; Aldubhani et al., 2022). Also, the investigation by Singh et al. (2017) which employs the meta-analysis method confirms the negative association between aggressive working capital policy and profitability.

Therefore, it is interesting, if the demographic characteristics of managers play an important role in decisions regarding working capital policy. One should expect that managers' propensity to avoid risky decisions might result in applying a more conservative working capital management approach. This assumption was confirmed by researchers, who examined the impact of female directors on working capital management policy and profitability for the sample of Indonesian-listed companies (Nastiti et al., 2019) document that companies with female CFOs apply conservative investment policy. Despite this, the presence of a female CFO is positively related to the company's profitability. Also, the research from Pakistan companies reveals that a conservative working capital management policy is applied if the company has a higher level of board gender diversity (Khan et al., 2022). However, the moderate working capital management approach is associated with the financial expertise of the CFO.

2.2.2 *Age of executives and financial decisions*

Age is another dimension that may affect the behaviour of executives, especially strategic choices (Wiersema and Bantel, 1992). Researchers document that older directors are more experienced, more committed to the company, more likely to take a holistic approach, and less likely to make risky decisions. Younger directors are seen as more energetic and willing to implement innovative ideas (Koufopoulos et al., 2008; Anderson et al., 2011; Mishra and Jhunjhunwala, 2013). Older managers are more conservative which leads to a higher quality of financial reporting (Huang et al., 2012; Qi and Tian; 2012). Therefore, it is believed that the attitude towards risk and propensity to conservative choices of executives are associated with their age. Thus, the older directors are expected to make more conservative and less risky financial decisions. This association can be explained by a few reasons. First of all, the physical and mental energy of decision-makers decreases as they get older. Older executives also prefer the organizational status quo and aim at keeping financial security (Ginesti et al., 2021). For example, the research of Peltomäki et al. (2021), including the S&P 1500 firms, gives evidence that firms run by older CEOs are less risky in terms of market-based firm risk measures (Peltomäki, 2021), which can be the effect of more conservative company's financial and investment policy.

The literature regarding the role of executives' age in the decision-making process is very limited. The research of Burney et al. (2021) for US companies reveals that if the company is run by an older CEO, the net operating working capital is higher. Meanwhile, the companies with younger CEOs are more likely to implement more aggressive working capital management policies, i.e. the level of inventory is lower and accounts payable are higher. It confirms the assumption, that younger directors due to their higher inclination to risky behaviours, are engaged in more risky financial decisions, while older ones are more prone to reduce the risk.

The investigation for Belgian privately held SMEs (Orens and Reheul, 2013) documents that older CEOs are more likely to accumulate cash reserves than companies with younger CEOs. This finding is in line with the precautionary motive of holding cash. The research of Wawryszuk-Misztal (2021a) reveals that as the percentage of management board members aged 45–54 increases, the cash held by companies decreases, but the age of board members is not associated with the leverage.

However, the investigation for the largest European listed companies contradicts the assumption that companies run by older CFOs are less likely to finance R&D projects. It provides evidence that managers' age is positively associated with a higher level of R&D investment, which means that older CFOs are more likely to make more risky financial decisions (Ginesti et al., 2021).

2.2.3   Education of executives and financial decisions

According to human capital theory education and training skills can increase productivity. The higher level of education of executives improves their cognitive abilities, allows them to absorb new ideas (Naranjo-Gil et al., 2009), and affects their decision-making process as it provides tools for solving organizational problems (Xiong, 2016). The literature provides evidence that the education of managers is an important predictor of financial reporting quality. For example, CEOs with MBA degrees reveal more financial information (Lewis et al., 2014). Other researchers document that more educated managers are less likely to manage earnings (Xiong, 2016) and more likely to issue high-quality financial statements (Ran et. al. 2015). It is also reported that a higher level of education is associated with more ethical behaviour of managers (Troy et al., 2011).

The research of Ginesti et al. (2021) reveals that CFOs holding a Master of Business Administration (MBA) or Doctor of Philosophy (PhD) degree are more likely to increase their R&D investment. Since an R&D investment decision is a risky decision, one can expect that the propensity to make risky financial decisions increases as the level of education of the CFO is higher. The higher propensity to more risky behaviours of executives with MBA degrees is also confirmed by Frank and Goyal (2007). They document that companies with CFOs holding MBA degrees have a higher level of leverage. Also, the investigation of Polish companies provides evidence that the presence on the management board of at least one person with an MBA degree increases the use of liabilities by a company (Wawryszuk-Misztal, 2021a).

2.2.4   Experience of decision-maker and financial decisions

As professional experience has a multidimensional nature, many proxies are used to reflect the professional experience of decision-makers: tenure, international experience, accounting or auditing-related professional experience, and experience working as a scientist (Khalid et al., 2022).

The tenure of the CFO – the number of years the officer has been the CFO for the firm – is usually used as a proxy of its professional experience reflects the individual knowledge, abilities, managerial power, and reputation of the CFO and affects the value of human capital (Liu et al., 2022). A large body of research examines the association between CFO tenure and accounting policy choices (Muttakin et al., 2019; de Almeida and Lemes, 2020) or inclination to the ethical behaviour of an organization (Sun and Rakhman, 2013). The organizational behaviour theory provides two opposite views on this association. On the one hand, a CFO with longer tenure is more prone to restrain from activities that might destroy its reputation in the market. This assumption is confirmed by an investigation of S&P 500 Index companies, which reveals that CFOs with longer tenure are more likely to take CSR activities

(Sun and Rakhman, 2013). Also, the examination for Australian listed companies documents that if the CFO has a longer tenure in the organization, a more conservative approach to accounting policy is applied (Muttakin et al., 2019). All of these activities allow the CFO to maintain or increase the reputation.

On the other side, the longer tenure of CFOs ensures them greater power in the organization and thus enables them to choose more aggressive accounting policies (Muttakin et al., 2019). This assumption was also confirmed by research on Australian companies – the longer tenure of the CFO as a member of the board is associated with more aggressive accounting practices (Muttakin et al., 2019). Thus, CFO tenure in the organization might affect the financial decisions. The investigation of Frank and Goyal (2007) including CEOs and CFOs from US public companies for the period of 1993–2004 reveals that leverage is affected by CFO's characteristics rather than CEO's. The longer the tenure of CFO the lower leverage is. However, higher leverage is observed if the CFO has previously worked in a financial institution (Frank and Goyal, 2007).

The study for Chinese companies analyses if corporate cash holding is affected by management team tenure (Cai and Li, 2022). The larger cash reserves are holed if the CEO and CFO have the same tenure. These findings confirm the assumption that managers with the same tenure communicate more effectively, i.e. a lower cost of communication is expected and a greater probability of reaching an agreement. The CFO with the same tenure as the CEO is likely to contribute CEO's strategic decisions and motivation for holding excessive cash (Cai and Li, 2022).

Dittmar and Duchin (2016) reveal how managerial attitude towards risk evaluates throughout a career. They document that both the CFO's and the CFO's previous professional experience play an important role in the decision-making process. They conclude that if the manager worked in a company that experienced trouble, he is more likely to avoid risk. Thus, the more conservative financial policies are followed by the current company, i.e. indebtedness is lower, the cash reserves are higher, and capital expenditures are limited (Dittmar and Duchin, 2016).

Other researchers examine how the accounting background of a CFO affects financial policy. Hoitash et al. (2016) document that companies operating in high-grow industries and with "accounting" CFOs refrain from R&D investments, capital expenditures, and external financing. Thus, as a result of such conservative behaviour, the negative association between accountant CFO in high-industry company and firm value is observed. The results for low-growth industries reveal that an accountant CFO has a positive effect on firm value. However, the accounting background of the CFO is not significantly associated with cash holdings, both in high-growth and low-growth industries (Hoitash et al., 2016).

Another dimension of managerial experience is internationalization. It can be defined as international education and international work experience.

Existing literature documents that a higher level of top manager internationalization contributes to better management in companies that operate in different and complex environments. It also fosters the choice of international corporate strategy and then succeeds in national and international markets (Dauth et al., 2017). Taking the perspective of upper echelons and human capital theory, the internationalization of managers is an important factor affecting company outcomes. Nielsen (2010) states that foreign-born executives possess the knowledge about culture, behaviour, and norms of foreign countries, which is the source of knowledge about conducting business abroad. International experience develops unique skills, creates international networks, and broads the managers' worldview (Le and Kroll, 2017). Thus, a CFO with international experience has a higher propensity to make risky decisions and choose aggressive financial policy. However, according to the authors' knowledge, this assumption has not been analysed yet.

2.3　CFO demographic characteristics and firms performance

A large body of research documents that the demographic characteristics of executives, and especially the demographic diversity of executives' teams affect the company's performance. Theoretical rationales for appointing diversified executives' teams are provided by many theoretical conceptions such as agency theory, resource dependence theory, human capital theory, and social capital theory. Since more diversified executive teams provide a company with different knowledge, relationships, experience, etc., the higher firms' performance is expected. Contrary to this, theories developed by social psychology – self-categorization theory (Turner, 1985) and social identity theory (Tajfel and Turner, 1979; 1986) give arguments against board diversity. The higher diversity of management teams results in problems with communication and conflicts, which in turn reduces the team's effectiveness and firm performance.

Based on the above theoretical assumption, many researchers investigate if there is a business case for board gender diversity, and give arguments for or against women's inclusion into management teams (Adams and Ferreira, 2009; Kim and Lim, 2010; Terjesen et al., 2016). Furthermore, some studies confirm the positive association between board diversity in terms of age and performance (Mahadeo et al., 2012; Ararat et al., 2015). However, one should point out that the empirical results on the role of board diversity for company performance are mixed (see, e.g. Martin-Ugedo and Minguez-Vera, 2014; Marinova et al., 2016; Simionescu, 2021).

Only a few studies focus on the role of CFO characteristics for a firm's performance. The reason for this is that traditionally the CFO was responsible for overseeing the financial aspects. Since the CFO's scope of responsibilities includes also shaping and executing strategy (Datta and Iskandar-Datta, 2014), the association between the CFO's characteristics (gender, age, education, and experience) and financial performance would be significant.

The research for Chinese companies reveals a positive association between female CFOs and performance, but this relationship is significant for companies in low-growth industries. However, such an association is not significant for high-grow industries. The rationale for that is that companies with growth opportunities and female CFOs reject high-risk projects which might increase financial performance (Han et al., 2020).

The investigation of Girigori (2013) for the sample of 395 S&P 500 firms reveals that CFO expertise is related to a firm's performance. The profitability of a company is higher if the CFO has worked in the current company before being appointed to the CFO position. However, a CFO with a master's degree in business administration and experience in other industries contributes to lower profitability.

The association between the financial expertise of CFOs and earnings per share was investigated by Rubin (2017) for 403 small US companies included in the Russell 2000 Index. The age of CFOs and the CFO's CPA licensure status were applied as a proxy of financial expertise. The results of this study provide arguments for hiring CFOs with financial expertise.

The investigation of Datta et al. (2023) based on the hand-collected data on the CFO's prior experience and educational profile documents the influence of CFOs' on firms' performance measured as market return. Both positive market reactions to CFO's appointment and post-hiring firm's performance are observed in some circumstances, i.e. the company appoints an "elite" CFO and the company is small and has high growth opportunities. The "elite" CFOs are people with strategically oriented and scarce human capital which is the result of prior experience and elite educational background. This study gives evidence that CFO characteristics are important for investors, as they are likely to buy shares of the company with the elite CFO (Datta et al., 2023).

2.4 CFO power and financial decisions

Analysing the association between the CFO's individual characteristics and financial decisions or firm performance, another attribute of the CFO, i.e. CFO power, should be included in the research. The rationale behind this decision arises from the assumption that only the CFO with great authority has a real influence on financial decisions. If CFOs are powerful, their personal attitude towards risk and overconfidence might be important for financial decisions. In another case, the personal characteristics of the CFO, both reflected by direct and indirect measures of risk attitude, are not important in explaining the CFO's role in the decision-making process.

2.4.1 The dimensions of CFO power

The literature on top management decisions emphasizes the role of managerial power which is considered as the central issue in strategic decisions.

Powerful persons can force their will (Finkelstein, 1992). Finkelstein points out four dimensions of top managers' power: structural power, ownership power, expert power, and prestige power. The origin of structural power is formal organizational structure which allows the manager to influence others. Ownership power is the result of managerial shareholdings, that give the manager a tool of control over other board members, who are not company owners. What is more, the power of a manager is also reinforced if he is a founder of a company. Expert power is based on the managerial ability to cope with environmental contingencies. Since the manager creates relationships with stakeholders, he allows the company to gain success. Another source of managerial power is prestige power. It is the personal prestige or status of the manager, which facilitates to gain of valuable information from the institutional environment (Finkelstein, 1992).

The literature provides some measures of CFO power such as board membership (i.e. insider/executive director), family membership, company ownership, tenure in the organization, tenure as a CFO, or measures including the CFO's compensation (Florackis and Sainani, 2018). However, there is an opinion that managerial power is a multidimensional concept and thus it requires complex measure (i.e. index power) which includes many dimensions of managerial power (Finkelstein, 1992; Sheikh, 2019). For example, Florackis and Sainani (2018) constructed the CFO power index that is based on variables regarding the CFO's attributes such as being an executive director, holding a professional certification in accounting or finance, and the CFO's compensation.

Another example is the CFO Influence Index constructed by Ferris and Sainanni (2021). It includes the following variables: CFO board membership, CFO outside directorship (i.e. if the CFO is a non-executive director in other firms), variables reflecting the CFO's position among senior managers (i.e. two variables referring to the CFO's relative compensation), CFO seniority (CFO's age), CFO M&A experience (the number of M&A transactions the CFO had been involved), CFO financial expertise (i.e. if CFO holds a chartered qualification). All of these seven measures were converted into dummy variables and then summed to obtain the CFO influence index, which takes values from 0 to 7 (i.e. from the least to highest CFO power). This index was used to capture if the CFO's personal characteristics are important for decisions regarding M&A in the UK-listed companies (Ferris and Sainanni, 2021).

There are strong rationales behind including in the power index the above variables reflecting CFO power. CFO's board membership allows to make connections with other members of the board, especially the CEO (Adams and Ferreira, 2007; Bedard et al., 2014). This statement arises from the friendly board theory (Adams and Ferreira, 2007) and social network theory (Bedard et al., 2014). According to these theoretical concepts, being a member of the board provides access to detailed company data and the possibility of frequent personal meetings. As a result, the CFO as a member of the board might create friendly relationships with other board members (Bedard et al., 2014). Other measures such as CFO age, tenure, and expertise reflect the value of social and human capital that the CFO possesses, and thus, the ability to influence the company's behaviour.

2.4.2 CFO power, financial decisions, and firm performance

The research on the CFO's power role in financial decisions or performance is very limited. The researchers usually focus their attention on the CEO power's dimensions and its impact on the company's behaviour (see Korkeamäki et al., 2017; Sheikh, 2019).

There are examples of investigations on the CFO's power impact on the cash holdings decisions. The research of Mobbs (2018) for a sample of non-financial S&P 1500 firms from 1997 to 2014 provides evidence that CFOs' board membership ensures them a greater impact on financial policy in comparison with external financial expertise. There are differences between companies with and without CFOs on the board. If the CFO is on the board, the cash is managed more effectively, i.e. the cash reserves are lower. However, during the financial crisis, the cash holdings in companies with CFOs on the board were higher than in companies with external CFOs. Thus, being a member of the board means a greater authority of the CFO and increases the CFO's impact on financial decisions (Mobbs, 2018).

Also, the research of Florackis and Sainani (2018) for UK companies reveals that the level of cash holdings depends on the CFO's power. They constructed the CFO power index and then identified the companies with "strong" and "weak" CFOs. The results show that companies with strong CFOs hold lower cash reserves. It results from the fact that strong CFOs have weak precautionary motives for holding cash and they are inclined to perform the monitoring role (Florackis and Sainani, 2018).

Since being a member of the board is a dimension of CFO power, the impact of the CFO position on financial performance is also analysed in the literature. Two opposite views explain how CFO membership might influence the company's performance. Taking the perspective of the agency theory, the CFO as a member of the board has greater influence on company policy (Finkelstein, 1992). The more powerful CFO (i.e. insider on the board) contributes to lower independence of the board, thus the monitoring role of the board might be reduced leading to lower effectiveness (Duong et al., 2020). According to the friendly board theory (Adams and Ferreira, 2007), since the CFO provides additional information, the advisory role of the board is performed more effectively. Consequently, an increase in performance is expected. The investigation of Australian companies gives evidence that CFO membership negatively affects the company's performance and earnings quality (Duong et al., 2020). This result is in line with agency theory, which allows us to conclude that the CFO as a member of the board reduces the board's monitoring role.

Another aspect of CFOs' power is their family membership. According to prior research, when a family company grows and becomes larger and older, it turns to non-family experts, especially non-family CFOs. What is more, usually the non-family CFO is the first manager in a company, who is not a family member (Lutz and Schraml, 2012; Hiebl, 2013a). The most important rationale behind the decision to hire non-family financial experts is the financial knowledge and experience provided by this person. For example, the research for German companies points out that non-family CFOs are more likely to use more advanced financial management techniques than companies with family CFOs (Lutz et al., 2010; Hiebl, 2013b). Thus, the companies with non-family CFOs are expected to have better performance than the companies with family CFOs, which was empirically confirmed.

The investigation of Italian small- and medium-sized companies (Caselli and Di Giuli, 2010) documents that the family CFO is negatively associated with return on assets and return on investment. It means that companies with non-family CFOs have better performance than those with family CFOs. What is more, the firm's performance is stronger if the company has both a family CEO and a non-family CFO (Caselli and Di Giuli, 2010). Similar results for Italian small- and medium-sized family firms are reported by Gordini (2016). These results give support for resource dependence theory and emphasize the great meaning of financial advice provided by non-family CFOs.

Taking the perspective of upper echelons theory, which suggests that top managers affect the firm's strategic choices, the interesting issue is the question if non-family CFOs are more powerful than those from family.

The research including non-family CFOs hired by Australian small- and medium-sized family companies reveals that the financial expertise of a CFO is not fully utilized. The interviewed non-family financial managers admitted, that they could be more involved in strategic planning, whereas they are mostly concerned with key financial and accounting issues. What is more, family companies are more likely to use the knowledge of external financial advisors than non-family CFOs, to handle difficult financial issues (Gurd and Thomas, 2012). Similarly, Hiebl (2013a) provides a theoretical assumption that non-family CFOs in family companies provide financial advice to the family CEO who makes strategic decisions.

To sum up, on the one hand, non-family CFO is rather "bean counter "rather than a person responsible for making strategic choices, but on the other hand, a non-family CFO contributes to a firm's performance as she or he applies more advanced financial management techniques.

The literature also points out that the CFO plays an important in the M&A process. The rationale for this statement is that the CFO is involved in the selection process, providing the financing, risk, and return assessment (Iskandar-Datta and Shekhar, 2020). In particular, the CFO's power is considered to be an important factor in the M&A process. While some researchers report that CFO power provides better post-acquisition performance (Florackis and

Sainani, 2018), others document that a more powerful CFO decreases the acquisition premiums and increases the M&A announcements return, but does not affect post-acquisition performance (Keck and Tang, 2016).

***

To sum up, since the role of CFOs is growing, the larger impact of CFOs on financial policy and company performance is expected. However, prior research regarding this issue is very limited. Our investigation makes some contributions to behavioural finance literature.

In existing literature, the description of managers' impact on financial decisions and firm performance mostly refers to the CEO. However, the CFO as a member of the top management team taking part in the decision process should be included in the research. Additionally, most of the research implements indirect measures of attitude towards risk (demographic characteristics and overconfidence). However, direct measures to identify attitudes towards risk apart from demographic characteristics and overconfidence should be considered.

What is more, existing empirical research gives evidence, that there is an extra factor affecting the role of CFO – CFO power. There are some CFOs' attributes that make them more or less powerful. Since CFO power is a multidimensional and complex issue, the researchers use many different measures of CFO power - from those reflecting demographic characteristics (gender and age), through attributes related to education and experience, and ending with features related to the position held in the company. In our research, the CFO power using variables referring to the CFO position in the current company (e.g. board membership, CFO ownership) was implemented in the research.

However, some attributes of powerful CFOs interact with their demographic characteristics and thus determine the CFO's behaviour, financial policy choices, and performance. It happens because, the sources of CFO power are rooted in both his/her demographic characteristics such as gender, age, experience, education, and the CFO's position in the current company (board membership, shareholdings, and family membership).

3 Research design and sample characteristics

3.1 The research model and hypotheses development

Knowing the research gap on the CFO role, the research aimed at investigating the CFO in a comprehensive way was prepared. It attempts to unveil the demographic characteristics of the CFOs (such as gender and age), their expertise (educational background and professional expertise), their individual traits (such as overconfidence), their attitude towards risk, their scope of duties and responsibilities, their position in the company structure, their power, and actual impact on the most important issues in the company.

The research is based on the assumption that differences in the risk attitude of CFOs are rationales for differences in financial policy and performance of surveyed firms. Therefore, the research is to find out the relationship between the CFOs' characteristics and financial decisions (cash holdings and capital structure), and then to analyse if the CFOs' individual characteristics are associated with the firm's financial performance. Thus, the following hypothesis was formulated:

H1: The CFO risk attitude is associated with financial decisions and financial performance.

Contrary to prior literature which usually applies demographic dimensions of executives to capture their risk attitude, the research uses both: indirect (demographic characteristics and overconfidence) and direct measures. To measure the psychological dimensions of CFOs (i.e. the level of risk aversion), the survey questionnaire was built (which is described in detail in Section 3.2). The questionnaire was also used to get information CFOs' personal characteristics. Additionally, the research is expected to find which measures of CFOs' risk attitude (direct vs. indirect) are better predictors of executives' choices. Therefore, it allows us to formulate the following hypotheses:

H1a: The indirect measures of CFO risk attitude are associated with financial decisions and financial performance.
H1b: The direct measure of CFO risk attitude is associated with financial decisions and financial performance.

DOI: 10.4324/9781003473190-4

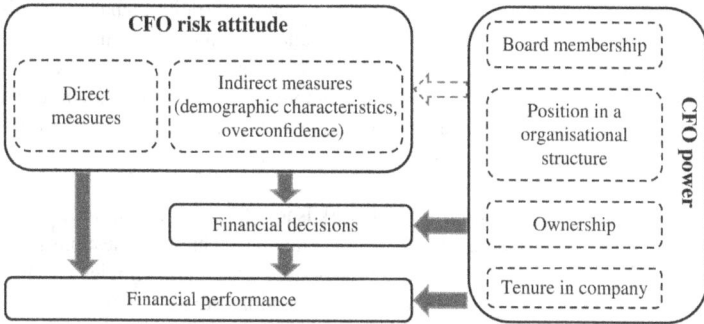

Figure 3.1 The research model

Apart from CFO risk attitude (coming from direct and indirect features), CFO power as a factor affecting the impact on financial decisions was included in our research. The CFO power might come from different characteristics: being a co-owner of the company, being a member of the management board etc. Despite the CFOs' risky attitude (due to personal characteristics or overconfidence), the actual CFO impact might be limited to traditional functions (due to low CFO power). To capture the real impact of the CFO on financial decisions, the set of variables that reflects the CFO's power was employed (see Section 5.2). Since the impact of CFOs on financial decisions might be disturbed by their low power, what conditions must be met to find the CFO affects the financial decisions. Thus, the following hypothesis was formulated:

H2: The CFO's power affects financial decisions and financial performance.

The research model for our study is presented in Figure 3.1.

3.2 Survey questionnaire

The main tool that was adopted to get information on CFOs was a survey questionnaire. The main source of information on financial data of the companies that CFOs come from was the EMIS database.

The survey approach allows us to ask many unique questions. We use a survey-based approach to provide new insight into the people and processes behind corporate decisions. This method allows us to address issues that traditional empirical work based on large archival data sources cannot. For example, via the survey, it is possible to get information on personality, gauge risk aversion, and measure other behavioural phenomena. This mode of inquiry is similar to those of experimental economists (who often administer gambling experiments) and psychologists (who administer psychometric tests). There are few studies attempting to measure the attitudes of senior management directly through personality tests. The survey quantifies the behavioural traits of senior executives and also harvests information related to career paths, education, and demographics. We also ask questions related to standard corporate finance decisions such as leverage policy, debt maturity, and acquisition activity. This allows us to relate attitudes and managerial attributes to corporate actions.

A common approach used in prior work is to infer executive attitudes from observed executive actions. While this is a laudable technique, questions arise about the validity of the action as a broad-based proxy, and samples are limited to companies for which such managerial actions are observable. A different approach was adopted, in which managers' personality traits and attitudes were identified using well-established questions. These questions have been shown in psychology and economics to be valid measures of people's attitudes. The attitudes of senior management were measured directly through personality tests and related them to firm-level policies.

The companies that have a stable board of directors composition and the same person as the CFO over the 2019–2020 period were contacted. A survey consisting of 25 questions on several groups of issues was constructed.

The first issue we investigate is connected with demographic characteristics, such as age and gender.

Investigation of gender in financial decisions has a quite long history. Research on board gender composition has appeared in academic journals since the early 1980s. Since the mid-2000s, the gender of directors has garnered significant interest from scholars. Studies of women directors as individuals are important because they allow us to develop an accurate portrayal of this group of women. Not only can this help us establish what kinds of women succeed in accessing board positions, but it is also a prerequisite for refining arguments about the effects of women on boards. Research on gender frequently assumes that besides their gender as a readily observable aspect of diversity women directors bring other, not readily observable aspects of diversity to boards – that they systematically differ from men concerning their knowledge, skills, abilities, experiences, attitudes, values, personality traits, behavioural styles, and so on. In other words, gender is used as a proxy for other heterogeneity constructs (Kirsch, 2018).

Another dimension of demographic characteristics – age – attracts the attention of many researchers. People having different ages also have different cognitive abilities and shared values (De Meulenaere et al.,2016). Younger people, when compared to elders, find it easier and faster to develop new skills. They have higher adaptability to new situations and new technologies (Bugg et al., 2006). They are more energetic and less risk-averse (Herrmann and Datta, 2005). Elder people, on the other hand, have more wisdom and abilities to solve problems. They are more cautious and wish to remain "status quo" (Talavera et al., 2018).

Hambrick and Mason (1984) assume that demographic characteristics determine strategic decisions and in the results firm performance. Many researchers indicate that diversity in demographic characteristics brings several benefits for the companies: ethical and economic (Brammer et al., 2007; Seierstad, 2016). The second issue we investigate is connected to educational background. To detect the educational background of the CFO the questions on the level of education, the field of education, additional courses, and education abroad were asked.

Educational background is perceived as the proxy reflecting human capital value (Darmadi, 2013). Education background might be assessed through the level of education (e.g. higher school or Ph.D. studies) and the field of education (e.g. technical or financial education). Educational background affects cognitive abilities: the ability to process information and the way the decisions are taken. It affects how individuals behave in uncertainty and make complex decisions. A higher level of education is connected with social status, social network, and professional career development (Anderson et al., 2011). People with higher levels of education are convinced that the changes are necessary, they are able to process a great deal of information quickly, and they have abilities to recognize signals coming from the environment (Camelo et al., 2010).

Wawryszuk-Misztal (2021a) believes that companies benefit from employing people with higher education and with diversity in the field of education (e.g. mixed team of technicians and economists). Milliken and Martins (1996) believe that diversity in the field of educational background increases access to resources, increases the scope of alternative options, and increases the quality of decisions. However, the diversity in the field of education might lead to conflicting situations due to different perceptions, attitudes, and reactions to difficult situations.

The third issue we investigate is connected with professional experience. To detect the professional experience of the CFO the questions on: work for the current company, the professional experience in the CFO position, and previous professional experience were asked. To get knowledge on the work for the current company, the questions on the number of years the CFO works for the company and the first position they took when they got a job at the current company were asked. The questions on how long they are in the position of CFO not only in the current company but in general and the number of companies (except the current company) they were in the CFO positions were also asked. The questions on the previous professional experience: type of the company they have work before joining the current company – especially to detect whether they come from e.g. Big4 or financial institutions, experience as the member of the board of directors or supervisory board – in a private or public company, and in non-profit organization were asked. Additionally, a question on foreign professional experience was asked.

Several theories emphasize the role of professional experience: upper echelons theory, agency theory, and resource-based theory. According to the theory, professional experience is a necessary attribute of each member of the board – of directors and supervisory (Gray and Nowland, 2017). Having wide and diverse professional experience allows one to look at issues from various perspectives, and to use a wide scope of cognitive resources, offering more alternative options (Harjoto et al., 2018). Additionally, Polish companies when introducing the diversity policy focus on professional experience. Wawryszuk-Misztal (2021b) found that the explanations provided by 152 companies reveal that competence, experience, and qualifications are the most important criteria for appointing board members, and, consequently, gender and age are not important dimensions (59 companies).

Another part of the survey was aimed at identifying the role of the CFO in financial decision-making.

Graham et al. (2015) show how the magnitude of delegation varies across the key corporate policies, and whether the sensitivity of delegation varies across policies and key drivers of those policies. Thus, a question on how CFO perceive their role in decision-making in creating strategy and long-term plans, investment decisions, raising capital, shaping the terms and conditions of paying for supplies, shaping the terms and conditions of getting payment from clients, cash surplus management, expenditures of company's other departments, choosing the methods of presentations business activities in financial statement, and timeliness of financial statement was asked (with a 1–5 Likert scale where 1 is the lowest impact and 5 is the biggest impact).

The previous question refers to the subjective CFO perception of their role in the company. The next questions in our survey were formulated to reveal the scope of CFO responsibilities in the company. There are situations that CFO might perceive themselves as having a low impact on financial decisions and be blamed for the financial decisions' results (Friedman, 2014). The question on how CFOs perceive their responsibility in decision-making in creating strategy and long-term plans, investment decisions, raising capital, financial liquidity management, financial firm performance and company's profitability, choosing the methods of presentation of business activities in financial statements, and timeliness of financial statement was asked (with a 1–5 Likert scale where 1 is the lowest responsibility and 5 is the biggest responsibility).

As the two questions above reflect the subjective perceptions, we attempt to find the real role of the CFO in the company. That is why we ask questions on time spent on specific types of activities. To find out the actual role of the CFO, we use the Deloitte approach assuming four roles of the CFO: Steward, Operator, Strategist, and Catalyst (Deloitte, 2007; Carson, 2012; Canace, 2014). The division of time of CFOs interaction with their CEOs and other business units might allow them to identify the real role of the CFO. That is why a question on which type of everyday activities is the most and the least time-consuming was asked.

Another set of questions is to unveil the real role, position, and power of the impact of the CFO in the company against other directors; especially the CEO and general ledger. A question on the share of the current company capital the CFO and their families hold was asked. The higher the stake the stronger the CFO role and impact (Javeed and Lefen, 2019). A question on the CFO position in the company structure, especially whether the CFO is a member of the board of directors was included in the survey. The CFO as the board member has a stronger impact (Duong et al., 2020). A question about who the general ledger reports to: directly to the CEO, directly to the CFO was asked. If the principal accounting officer reports directly to the CEO skipping the CFO, the weaker position of the CFO in the company (Doron et al., 2019).

The last set of questions refers to personal traits (especially attitude towards risk) and individual cognitive biases (especially overconfidence).

Following Graham et al. (2013), the identification of the personal risk-aversion attitude was conducted by asking question on the CFO's attitude towards financial issues such as planning, investment decisions, financing, cash holdings, inventory management, and voluntary disclosures. They were asked to follow their own feelings not connected with the actual situation of the company they work for. They are expected to choose one out of two options. If they choose more "b" answers they reflect a more risk-averse attitude.

The last part of the survey is devoted to CFO overconfidence. It is quite challenging to identify overconfidence. This becomes an especially evident problem when it comes to managers. Usually, in cognitive psychology, overconfidence is identified when surveying people. But when referring to managers, other ways of identifying overconfidence were developed. By far the most influential proxies for managerial overconfidence have been constructed by Malmendier and Tate (2005), whose proxies and datasets have been used in many other studies into overconfidence: based on options (longholder, holder 67), shares (net buyer), and based on press articles. Another method of identifying managerial overconfidence was first proposed by Lin et al. (2005). They argued that overconfident managers were apt to make upwards-biased earnings forecasts. If there are more upwards biases than those downwards biases, the managers are regarded as overconfident. The method based on the frequency of M&A made by managers was proposed first by Doukas and Petmezas (2007). They argued that the more confident a manager is, the higher the frequency of M&A. They regarded a manager as overconfident if they made at least five M&As during the study period. The method based on manager's relative compensations was proposed first by Hayward and Hambrick (1997). They argued that the higher the manager's relative compensation to other managers is, the more important the manager's position, and consequently, they would be apt to be overconfident. They used "the manager cash compensation divided by the second-highest-paid officer" in their measurement. The first problem with implementing the methods described above is that these methods allow evaluating overconfidence by behaviour, not by beliefs. And human behaviour might sometimes result from the strategy implemented by the company not from its managers' beliefs (e.g. frequency of M&A). Additionally, those measures might be applied to specific companies that pay with stock options, release forecasts, or the information about the manager's compensation – these are usually listed companies. Those measures cannot be implemented to identify overconfidence among private companies. For the sake of the research on overconfidence, the questions on their beliefs, attitudes, and perceptions were included in the survey. Wrońska-Bukalska (2016) approach was employed who developed a survey to detect overestimation, overplacement, and overoptimism.

Three questions were included in the survey questionnaire to detect all elements of overconfidence. Overestimation reflects how people assess their knowledge against an objective verifiable base. To detect overestimation, six questions on specific (in this case economics) knowledge were asked. The questions required to give answers "yes" or "no" (e.g. Is it legal to call the police if you believe that an employee is under the influence of alcohol?). Additionally, the participants were to point the confidence that they answered the question correctly by providing probability in the range between 50% and 100%.

Overplacement reflects how people assess their abilities against a subjective base (other people's abilities). To detect overplacement two questions how participants perceive a) themselves now and b) their future in comparison to others were asked. The possible answers were: better than 20%, better than 50%, and better than 80%.

Overoptimism reflects how people assess the probability of experiencing a negative (or positive) event. To detect overoptimism a question about outcomes (e.g. "my results are usually better than I expect"), attributing successes and failures (e.g. "my success is due to me"), planning fallacy (e.g. "I always implement my plans no matter what happens"), betting on own abilities in random events (e.g. "I bet the results according to my knowledge") were asked. For each question there was an opposite one ("my results are worse than I expect", "my success is due to a good luck", "while implementing plans I always monitor the environment whether it is still worth implementing", and "I bet the result at random") to check consistency of the response. The answers (a) point more overoptimism while (b) point less overoptimism.

3.3   Sample characteristics

We sent the survey questionnaire to a great number of CFOs. However, there is a big reluctance among business practitioners to provide answers and be involved in the research. As a result, we got 155 answers. The distribution of our sample is presented in Tables 3.1–3.25.

In our sample, there are 79 men and 76 women. The sample is divided almost in half as for the gender criteria.

In our sample, the average age is 47 years old.

Tables 3.3–3.6 present the sample distribution in terms of education. We asked questions on the level and type of education but also on additional education and education abroad.

We find that 98% of the sample graduated from university studies. Only two persons got only secondary school education (below bachelor level) and another two persons got a Ph.D.

We find 93% of the sample finished their studies in the field of management and economics sciences. Only four persons got law and administration education and six persons technical education.

Table 3.1 Gender distribution of the sample

Specification	No.	%
Male	79	51
Female	76	49

Table 3.2 Age distribution of the sample

Specification	No.	%
Under 35	7	5
Between 36–45	56	36
Between 46–55	64	41
Between 56–65	25	16
Above 66	3	2

Table 3.3 Distribution of the sample in terms of the level of education

Specification	No.	%
Secondary school	2	1
B.a./m.a.,	151	98
Ph.D. Level	2	1

Table 3.4 Distribution of the sample in terms of the field of education

Specification	No.	%
Management and economics	145	93
Law and administration	4	3
Technical education	6	4

Table 3.5 Distribution of the sample in terms of additional education

Specification	No.	%
Postgraduate studies	82	53
MBA courses	19	12
Certified accountant, CIMA, CFA, ACCA	27	17
Certified auditor	65	42
Certified tax advisor, certified broker	4	3

Note: It was possible to indicate more than one answer that is why the sum of indications is higher than 100%.

Table 3.6 Distribution of the sample in terms of education abroad[a]

Specification	No.	%
One semester	5	3
Full cycle at bachelor or master level	7	5
Courses or trainings	22	14

Note: It was possible to indicate more than one answer that is why the sum of indications is higher than 100%.

Out of the total sample, there are 140 people (90% of the sample) that got additional education after graduating the university studies. However, the number and percentage are more than 155 and 100% as there are a lot of people that got several additional courses and certificates. This additional education includes postgraduate studies in the field of finance and accounting (53%), and courses that ended with an auditor certificate (42%). Less popular is having a certificate in CIMA, CFA, ACCA, or accounting (17%) and MBA (12%). There are only four persons (3%) of the sample that got certificates of tax advisor or broker.

We find 28 people (18%) having foreign education. However, the total number of indications is higher (34) as there are six people having at least two types of foreign education. The most popular foreign education is participation in courses and training abroad (14%). Less popular is studying at the foreign universities (8%).

We find one study that takes into account CFO education obtained abroad: Dauth, Pronobis, and Schmid (2017). They measure the number of years of higher education spent abroad. But they do not present the descriptive statistics and we cannot compare our findings with theirs.

The education gives a background for CFO professional experience. The professional experience of our sample is presented in Tables 3.7–3.12.

The average number of years of work for the current company is 11 with a median value of 10. Almost half of the respondents work for the current company up till nine years. But more than half of the sample has quite a long connection with the current company as they have worked for ten years or

Table 3.7 Distribution of the sample in terms of
the number of years of experience in the
current company

Specification	No.	%
Up till 9 years	74	48
10–19 years	54	35
20 years and more	27	17

Table 3.8 Distribution of the sample in terms of the
position the CFO got when started the job at
the current company

Specification	No.	%
Financial director	57	37
Managerial position	48	31
Financial specialist	50	32

Table 3.9 The relation between the number of years of experience in the current
company and the position the CFO got when started the job at the current
company

Specification	Total	Financial director	Managerial position	Financial specialist
Up till 9 years	74 (100%)	45 (61%)	15 (20%)	14 (19%)
10–19 years	54 (100%)	12 (22%)	24 (44%)	18 (34%)
20 years and more	27 (100%)	2 (7%)	8 (30%)	17 (63%)

Note: We present the number, and the share of the sample in % in parenthesis.

more. This might indicate a strong bond and loyalty to the company business
which gives strong power and authority.

When beginning work for the current company almost 40% of the respondents start their job as the financial director/CFO. Less than 1/3 of the sample
got managerial positions such as deputy financial director, general ledger, and

Table 3.10 Distribution of the sample in terms of
the number of years of experience in
the CFO position

Specification	No.	%
Up till 5 years	45	29
6–10	41	26
11–19 years	46	30
20 years and more	23	15

Table 3.11 Distribution of the sample in terms of
the number of companies that the
position of CFO was held (except for
the current company)

Specification	No.	%
1	35	23
2	25	16
3	19	12
4	6	4
5	4	1
6	2	1

Table 3.12 The relation between the number of years of experience in the CFO position
and the number of extra companies that the position of CFO was held

Years of experience	No. of CFOs	No. of CFOs holding CFO position				
		Only in current company	In 1 company	In 2 companies	In 3 companies	In 4 and more companies
Up till 5 years	45	26 (58%)	16 (35%)	3 (7%)	0	0
6–10	41	17 (41%)	8 (20%)	9 (22%)	5 (12%)	2 (5%)
11–19 years	46	18 (39%)	11 (24%)	6 (13%)	8 (17%)	3 (7%)
20 years and more	23 (100%)	3 (14%)	0 (0%)	7 (30%)	6 (26%)	7 (30%)

deputy general ledger. And less than 1/3 of the sample started as a financial
specialist such as analysts, cashiers, and accountants.

We find that the longer the respondent works for the current company the
lower position they got at the beginning – 63% of people working more than
20 years for the current company started their job as a specialist. But CFOs
working short for the company (less than ten years) got a higher position (financial director) at the beginning – 61% of people working less than ten years
for the current company started their job as a financial director/CFO.

The average number of years of experience in the CFO position is 11 with
a median value of 8. These numbers reflect both the current company but also
all previous workplaces. More than half of the sample held the CFO position
for less than ten years (55%). Almost half of the sample (45%) is CFO for
longer than ten years. It is worth mentioning that 15% of the sample (23 people) held the CFO position for longer than 20 years.

That is why we asked the question on the number of companies the respondent holds the CFO position except for the current company. We believe
that if there is more than one company the CFO position was held, a higher
professional experience is. However, a high number of companies might
mean a high turnover ratio which indicates a lower professional background.

For 64 respondents (42%), the current company is the first one they hold a CFO position. Half of the sample (51% and 79 people) hold the CFO position in less than four companies (apart from the current company). There are 12 people (6%) that got more experience than four companies.

We find that the longer the respondent works as the CFO the more companies they worked for – 86% of people working more than 20 years as the CFO work for two or more companies (not including the current company). However, respondents working quite short as the CFO has the lower experience – 58% of the sample working up to five years as the CFO worked for the current company only.

To identify the professional experience, we asked questions on the type of previous experience. Tables 3.13–3.16 present the sample characteristics in terms of previous professional experience.

Table 3.13 Distribution of the sample in terms of previous professional experience[a]

Specification	No.	%
Experience in work for accountancy office or audit company	49	32
Experience in work for Big4	7	4
Experience in work for financial institution such as bank or insurance company	33	17
Academic career	8	2

[a] It was possible to indicate more than one answer that is why the sum of indications is higher than 100%.

Table 3.14 Distribution of the sample in terms of the previous professional experience as a member of board of directors in other companies before joining current company (if applicable)[a]

Specification	No.	%
Yes – in a public/listed company	10	6
Yes – in a private company	42	25

[a] It was possible to indicate more than one answer that is why the sum of indications is higher than 100%.

Table 3.15 Distribution of the sample in terms of the previous professional experience as a member of supervisory board in other companies before joining current company

Specification	No.	%
Yes – in a public/listed company	11	7
Yes – in a private company	15	10

Table 3.16 Distribution of the sample in terms of previous professional experience abroad[a]

Specification	No.	%
Work for a company that is capitally linked to you current company	16	10%
Work for other company (not capitally linked to your current company)	12	8%

[a]   It was possible to indicate more than one answer that is why the sum of indications is higher than 100%.

We find that 70 people (46% of the sample) have no previous experience in specific types of companies. This does not mean that these people do not have professional experience at all, but they do not have experience in working e.g. Big4 or an audit company. There are 85 people (54% of the sample) with previous professional experience of a specific financial type. However, there are more indication (by 12) that indicates that there are several people with multiple specific financial previous experience.

We find that 107 people (69% of the sample) do not have previous experience connected with being a member of the board of directors. There are 48 people (31% of the sample) with such an experience. However, there are more indications (by 4) as there are four CFOs with experience as a member of a board of directors both in private and public companies.

We find that 129 people (83% of the sample) do not have previous experience connected with being a member of the supervisory board. There are 26 people (17% of the sample) with such an experience. Additionally, we find that 28 people have experience in being active members of non-profit organizations.

We find that 85% of the sample (131 people) has no working experience abroad. We find only 24 people (15% of the sample) who have working experience abroad. However, there are more than 24 indications as there are four people having multiple working experience abroad (work both for a company that is capitally linked to CFOs current company and not linked to the current company). Additionally, we find eight people (5%) with both education and work experience abroad.

The next set of questions was meant to reveal the CFO's real position and the power to impact the decision-making. As for sample CFOs and their family capital involvement in the share capital of the current company, we got an average of 6%. But only 17 people (11% of the sample) say that got a capital interest in the company while 138 people (89%) do not. Out of those 17 people, one person has a 50% stake in the company, another one 20%, and the rest (15 people) got less than 6% stake.

In our sample, 34% of the respondents are members of the board of directors, and 66% are not.

Table 3.17 Distribution of the sample in terms of the position of CFO in the company

Specification	No.	%
CFO as a financial director overseeing the financial department	103	66
CFO as a financial director and member of board of directors	40	26
CFO as a board member and another person as a financial director	12	8

Table 3.18 Distribution of the sample in terms of the person the chief accounting officer reports to

Specification	No.	%
directly to CEO	60	39
directly to CFO	85	55

We try to find out what is the position of CFO by investigating who the chief accounting officer reports to. If CAO reports to CFO, we think that the CFO position is stronger. We find 55% of cases in our sample that the CAO reports to the CFO. But we find 39% of cases that the CAO reports directly to the CEO skipping the CFO. Additionally, in six cases (4%) the financial director is the chief accounting officer and in four cases (2.5%) the company has no accountancy department (the accountancy department is outsourced).

Tables 3.19–3.22 refer to the role of the CFOs and their impact on financial decisions – both in terms of subjective perception and real-time spent on specific activities.

We find that the CFOs think that they have the strongest impact on raising capital, cash surplus management, and choosing the methods of presentations of business activities in financial statement and timeliness of financial statement (mean 4.5 and median 5.0). The next set of activities CFOs think they have an impact on are those connected with creating strategy and long-term plans, investment decisions, and expenditures of the company's other departments (a mean of 3.7–3.9 and a median of 4.0). There are two types of activities that CFOs think that they have quite high impact (above the middle of the 5-grade Likert scale) and these are impact on shaping the terms of the payment conditions to suppliers and from clients.

The answers on the perceived responsibilities are similar to those on the perceived impact on financial decisions. CFOs believe they are responsible to the greatest extent for raising capital, cash surplus management, and choosing the methods of presentation of business activities in financial statements and timeliness of financial statement (mean 4.5 and median 5.0). A similar

Table 3.19 Distribution of the sample in terms of the perceived impact on the financial decisions (from 1 to 5, where 1 is the lowest impact and 5 is the biggest impact)

Specification	1	2	3	4	5	Median	Mean
Creating strategy and long-term plans	4	12	26	70	43	4	3.9
Investment decisions (in fixed assets: property, plant and equipment, mergers, and acquisition)	6	19	31	66	33	4	3.7
Raising capital	4	1	12	30	108	5	4.5
Shaping the terms and conditions of paying for supplies	3	25	56	46	25	3	3.4
Shaping the terms and conditions of getting payment from clients	9	21	58	46	21	3	3.3
Cash surplus management	4	2	10	35	104	5	4.5
Expenditures of company's other departments	4	14	34	51	52	4	3.9
Choosing the methods of presentations of business activities in financial statement and timeliness of financial statement	4	4	6	34	107	5	4.5

meaning was appointed when the impact on financial decisions was investigated. The second important area of responsibility is this one connected with creating strategy and long-term plans, and investment decisions (a mean of 3.5–3.8 and a median of 4.0). A similar meaning was appointed again when the impact on financial decision was investigated. Responsibility for financial firm performance and the company's profitability was ranked quite high – above the middle of the 5 grade Likert scale (with a mean of 3.7 and a median of 4.0).

The subjective perception of the impact and responsibility for the financial decisions reflect a quite coherent picture: CFOs believe that they play an

Table 3.20 Distribution of the sample in terms of the perceived responsibilities for the results of the financial decisions (from 1 to 5, where 1 is the lowest responsibility and 5 is the biggest responsibility)

Specification	1	2	3	4	5	Median	Mean
Creating strategy and long-term plans	5	11	42	53	44	4	3.8
Investment decisions (in fixed assets: property, plant and equipment, mergers, and acquisition)	8	22	40	57	28	4	3.5
Raising capital	4	6	11	29	105	5	4.5
Financial liquidity maintenance	2	2	9	29	113	5	4.6
Choosing the methods of presentations of business activities in financial statement and timeliness of financial statement	4	3	12	35	101	5	4.5
Financial firm performance and company's profitability	5	9	46	60	35	4	3.7

Table 3.21 Distribution of the sample in terms of the time spent on CFO daily activities (from 1 to 4, where 1 is the most time-consuming and 4 is the least time-consuming)

Specification	1	2	3	4	Median	Mean
Strategy development, general aims formulating, strategic thinking – Strategist	27	36	61	31	3	2.6
Strategic and operational communication across the company, internal team creating and working on diverse projects – Catalyst	10	41	52	52	3	2.9
Day-to-day financial management, financial department management – Operator	65	39	19	32	2	2.1
Financial planning and analysis, financial reporting to CEO – Steward	67	43	23	22	2	2.0

important role in the decision-making process. To verify this perception, we asked questions about their daily routine.

Although the CFOs perceived their role mostly as strategic, their daily routine is mostly devoted to traditional activities. The highly ranked activities are those connected with preparing the financial information for CEO purposes – Steward (mean 2.0 and median 2) and day-to-day financial department management – Operator (mean 2.1 and median 2). Focus on these two roles reflects the traditional approach to the CFO role and financial policy development (Deloitte, 2007; Carson, 2012).

The next question was devoted to revealing the attitude towards risk (and risk aversion) in the financial decision-making process. More answers for (a) option reveal more acceptance of risky actions, while choosing option (b) reflects less risky attitude.

As for investment decisions (questions 1 and 2), more CFOs present risky attitude. More than 60% of respondents think that the investment decisions have the priority (and the financing should be adjusted to growth pace) while 35% think that the investment decision should be made within available funds. And 70% think that any time is good to implement an investment project (no matter what is the situation in the economic environment) while only 15% think that the investment decision should be timed and adjusted to the economic environment situation.

The risky attitude is also noticeable when inventory management is concerned – 63% of the respondents think that the inventory pool should be minimized while 25% think that the inventory stock should be higher to meet unexpected changes in the environment.

Quite a balanced attitude is presented when the capital structure and cash holdings are concerned. 40% of the respondents think that companies should rely on short-term financing to a greater extent while 41% point to long-term financing. 44% of the respondents think that the cash pool should be kept at a minimal level while 37% accept maintaining a higher precautionary level of the cash pool.

Table 3.22 Distribution of the sample in terms of the CFO attitude towards financial decision

Specification	Yes for (a)	Somewhere in the middle	Yes for (b)	Specification
1a) When creating plan, at the very beginning the investment spending is determined and then the capital should be found	94	7	54	1b) When creating plan, at the very beginning the available capital is determined and then the possible investment spending should be identified
2a) Every moment (even crisis) is good to implement profitable project no matter what the cash reserves are	108	23	24	2b) The profitable project should be implemented when having sufficient cash reserves and during economic boom
3a) When raising funds, the most important is to obtain them quickly no matter what is the cost of the funds	31	27	97	3b) When raising funds, the most important is to obtain them cheaply even if it takes more time
4a) Companies should use short-term financing (esp. trade credit)	62	30	63	4b) Companies should use long-term financing (esp. equity)
5a) The cash pool should be as low as possible due to its high opportunity cost	68	30	57	5b) The cash pool should be high due to future possible unpredictable events
6a) Companies should minimize the inventories due to their high maintenance costs	98	18	39	6b) Companies should have higher level of inventories in order to maintain the activity continuity
7a) When releasing voluntary disclosures, the company should publish information on specific events even if they are possible to occur	32	0	123	7b) When releasing voluntary disclosures, the company should publish information on specific events only after their occurrence

Risk aversion is noticeable when raising capital and voluntary disclosure are concerned. 63% of the respondents think that should be more cautious when raising funds, and the most important is to analyse and choose the funds cheaply even if it takes more time while 20% think that the cost of capital is of no importance, but the shortest time of getting the funds should be the priority. 79% of the respondents advocate for presenting only facts after the activities are accomplished while 21% allow to revealing the planned activities even if they are only possible to occur.

The next set of questions was meant to reveal the CFO's overconfidence. Tables 3.23–3.25 refer to the CFO overestimation, overplacement, and over-optimism – three components of overconfidence.

There is nothing wrong with not knowing the answer to the question. But when respondents give wrong answers and are quite sure that it is a proper answer indicates the overestimation. On the other side when respondents give the right answers and are not sure that it is proper indicates underestimation. Out of six questions, there are only two questions that most of the CFOs give wrong answers but they present similar certainty to those who give proper answers.

Pointing more "a" answers indicates more overoptimism while pointing more "b" answers indicates less overoptimism. The distribution shows that

Table 3.23 Distribution of the sample in terms of the overestimation

Specification	Proper answers	Average ratio of being sure with giving answer	Wrong answers	Average ratio of being sure with giving answer
Is it legal to dismiss worker who is on a sick leave?	55	92.8	100	92.3
Is it legal to arrange bookkeeping by accountancy office under task-specific contract?	136	88.6	19	68.9
Is it legal to ban smoking in a workplace?	140	92.2	15	87.3
Is it obligatory to report plans on gift lottery in a workplace to custom office?	98	88.4	57	70.0
Is it legal to call the police if you believe that an employee is under the influence of alcohol?	154	92.0	1	80.0
Does the documentation on transfer prices embrace only business entities/ entrepreneurs?	51	83.3	104	88.6

Table 3.24 Distribution of the sample in terms of the overoptimism

Specification	Yes for (a)	Somewhere in the middle	Yes for (b)	Specification
1a) My success is the result of my efforts	67	36	52	1b) My success is the result of good luck
2a) I always implement my plans no matter what happens	101	48	6	2b) There is no point in planning anything as something might go wrong and distort my plans
3a) I bet the results according to my knowledge	31	11	113	3b) I bet the results at random
4a) My business profits are always lower than I expect	24	56	75	4b) My business profits are always higher than I expect
5a) My failures in business are the results of other unpredictable situations and others people' misbehaviour	76	62	17	5b) Failures in business are the results of my mistakes

there are two statements with noticeable more "a" answers and two statements with noticeable more "b" answers. What is interesting, respondents think that their success is the result of both good luck and their efforts but their failures are due to other people's behaviour. They attribute their failures to other people. At the same time, they less optimistically predict future results as more people are surprised that the financial results are higher than they expected. At the same time, they are quite determined to implement their plans no matter what the circumstances.

As for overplacement, the respondents are quite moderate. Overplacement reflects how people assess their abilities against a subjective base (other people's abilities). If they pointed 80% that would mean that they place themselves in the top 20% of the managers.

Following Wrońska-Bukalska (2016), we estimated the overconfidence. This measure is based on overestimation, overoptimism, and overplacement. Based on data on overestimation, we calculated for each respondent

Table 3.25 Distribution of the sample in terms of the overplacement

Specification	80%	50%	20%	
I think I am better manager than	26	96	33	of other managers
I think my future will be better than the future of	26	91	38	of other managers

the average accuracy and the average certainty of giving answers. Then we calculated the difference between accuracy and certainty. If the difference was lower than −10% (accuracy was higher than certainty), we assigned −1 point. If the difference was between -9% and +9%, we assigned 0 points. If the difference was higher than 10% (accuracy lower than certainty), we assigned 1 point. Based on data on overoptimism, we assigned +1 points if the "a" answer was indicated and −1 if the "b" answer was indicated. Then we calculated each respondent's average ratio. Again, we assigned −1, 0, and +1 depending on the average: −1 for the lowest average, 0 and +1 for the highest average. Based on data on overplacement, we assigned +1 points if 80% was indicated, 0 for 50%, and −1 if 20% was indicated.

After adding all points assigned, we got the score for each respondent ranging from −3 to +3. Then we grouped CFOs into three groups – underconfident with scores −3 and −2; confident with scores −1, 0, and +1, and overconfident with scores +2 and +3. In our sample, we find 7 CFOs being underconfident, 98 (63% of the sample) confident, and 50 (32% of the sample) overconfident.

***

To identify the role and power of the CFO, we develop a survey. The role and power are described with several demographic characteristics: gender, age, but also their education, and experience.

We constructed a survey consisting of 25 questions on several groups of issues. Apart from demographic characteristics, we also try to detect the CFO's attitude towards financial decisions, the risk, and their role in company management. We sent the survey questionnaire to a great number of CFOs. However, there is a big reluctance among business practitioners to provide answers and be involved in the research. As a result, we got 155 answers.

Our sample is quite diversified in terms of age, gender, education, and experience of surveyed CFOs. However, our initial sample screening reveals the supportive role of the CFO being more operator and steward than a strategist and catalyst. We did not find any specific attitude towards risk-taking. Most of the surveyed CFOs are confident (with a small share of underconfident or overconfident CFOs in our sample).

4 The CFO profile and attitude towards financial decisions

4.1 The demographics characteristics of CFO risk attitude and CFO power

The main characteristics that affect financial decisions and financial performance are those reflected in the CFO risk attitude adjusted by CFO power. In our survey, we used both direct and indirect questions to identify CFO risk attitude. An indirect approach to CFO risk is reflected in e.g. age, or gender. A direct approach to CFO risk is reflected in question on the CFO attitude towards financial issues such as planning, investment decisions, financing, cash holdings, inventory management, and voluntary disclosures. In this part of the book, we present the relations between direct and indirect approach to CFO risk attitude and CFO power.

4.1.1 Gender and CFO risk attitude and CFO power

Since the literature documents that female directors provide the company with different skills, and experience than their male counterparts, we ask a question if there are differences in terms of risk attitude provided to the company by female and male CFOs.

Next, a couple of tables (Tables 4.1–4.8) reflect the CFOs' risk attitude both direct and indirect (overconfidence), and CFOs' gender.

All answers "a" reflect a more risky attitude while "b" is less risky. Women in five cases (out of seven) chose more risky answers, while men only in three cases chose more risky answers. These three cases are common for men and women and they refer to the priority to real plans, timing for implementing profitable projects, and minimizing inventories. The women are more risky when short-term financing is concerned and minimizing the cash pool. In case of short-term financing, there are only 43% of women presenting more risky attitude 30% hesitate whether to choose "a" or "b." But in two cases (short-term financing and cash pool), men are not definitely less risky as only 43% present a less risky attitude, another 30% present hesitation about whether to choose "a" or "b" and 30% choose a more risky attitude.

DOI: 10.4324/9781003473190-5

Table 4.1 Distribution of the sample in terms of the CFO attitude towards financial decision

Feature	Women	Men	
No.	76	79	
1a) When creating plan, at the very beginning the investment spending is determined and then the capital should be found	More a (47, 62%)	More a (47, 59%)	1b) When creating plan, at the very beginning the available capital is determined and then the possible investment spending should be identified
2a) Every moment (even crisis) is good to implement profitable project no matter what the cash reserves are	More a (56, 74%)	More a (52, 66%)	2b) The profitable project should be implemented when having sufficient cash reserves and during economic boom
3a) When raising funds, the most important is to obtain them quickly no matter what is the cost of the funds	More b (45, 59%)	More b (52, 66%)	3b) When raising funds, the most important is to obtain them cheaply even if it takes more time
4a) Companies should use short-term financing (esp. trade credit)	More a (33, 43%)	More b (34, 43%)	4b) Companies should use long-term financing (esp. equity)
5a) The cash pool should be as low as possible due to its high opportunity cost	More a (39, 51%)	More b (34, 43%)	5b) The cash pool should be high due to future possible unpredictable events
6a) Companies should minimize the inventories due to their high maintenance costs	More a (47, 62%)	More a (51, 65%)	6b) Companies should have higher level of inventories in order to maintain the activity continuity
7a) When releasing voluntary disclosures, the company should publish information on specific events even if they are possible to occur	More b (62, 82%)	More b (61, 77%)	7b) When releasing voluntary disclosures, the company should publish information on specific events only after their occurrence

Table 4.2 Gender and overconfidence

Specification	Women		Men	
	No.	%	No.	%
Underconfidence	2	3	5	6
Confidence	50	66	48	61
Overconfidence	24	31	26	33

Table 4.3 Gender and CFO membership in board of directors

Specification	Women		Men	
	No.	%	No.	%
CFO not a member of a board	54	71	49	62
CFO a member of a board	18	24	22	28
CFO as a board member and another person as a director of financial department	4	5	8	10

Table 4.4 Gender and distribution of the sample in terms of the person the chief accounting officer reports to

Specification	Women		Men	
	No.	%	No.	%
Chief accounting officer reports to CFO	31	41	54	68
Chief accounting officer reports to CEO	36	47	24	30
Others	9	12	1	2

Additionally, in those five cases that women present risky attitude, they are more risky than men. Women and men present less risky attitude in the other two cases – they prefer to raise funds cheaply even if it takes more time and to release voluntary disclosures only after their occurrence.

There are more confident CFOs among women (66%) than men (61%). Among men, there are more underconfident and overconfident CFOs.

Several next tables refer to the CFO power.

There are more women (71%) than men (62%) CFOs who are not a member of the board of directors. And there are more men (38%) than women (29%) that CFOs are members of the board of directors. This means that men enter or arrange their positions to be a member of the board of directors more often and make their positions firmer. This means that the source of power for men is being a member of the board of directors.

Table 4.5 Gender and stake in the current company

Specification	Women		Men	
	No.	%	No.	%
Yes	9	12	8	10
No	67	88	71	90
Median stake	2%	x	4%	x

Table 4.6 Gender and distribution of the sample in terms of the perceived impact on the financial decisions (from 1 to 5, where 1 is the lowest impact and 5 is the biggest impact)

Specification	Women		Men	
	Mean	Median	Mean	Median
Creating strategy and long-term plans	3.7	4	4.0	4
Investment decisions (in fixed assets: property, plant and equipment, mergers and acquisition)	3.6	4	3.7	4
Raising capital	4.4	5	4.7	5
Shaping the terms and conditions of paying for supplies	3.6	3.5	3.3	3
Shaping the terms and conditions of getting payment from clients	3.4	3	3.3	3
Cash surplus management	4.5	5	4.5	5
Expenditures of company's other departments	4.0	4	3.7	4
Choosing the methods of presentations of business activities in financial statement and timeliness of financial statement	4.5	5	4.6	3

There are more male (68%) than female (41%) CFOs that the chief accounting officer (CAO) reports to them. This means that men more often enter or arrange their positions to be reported to and make their positions firmer. This means that the source of power for men is their positions in company's structure.

Table 4.7 Gender and distribution of the sample in terms of the perceived responsibilities for the results of the financial decisions (from 1 to 5, where 1 is the lowest responsibility and 5 is the biggest responsibility)

Specification	Women		Men	
	Mean	Median	Mean	Median
Creating strategy and long-term plans	3.6	4	3.9	4
Investment decisions (in fixed assets: property, plant and equipment, mergers and acquisition)	3.5	4	3.5	4
Raising capital	4.3	5	4.6	5
Financial liquidity maintenance	4.5	5	4.7	5
Choosing the methods of presentations of business activities in financial statement and timeliness of financial statement	4.4	5	4.5	5
Financial firm performance and company's profitability	3.6	4	3.8	4

Table 4.8 Gender and distribution of the sample in terms of the time spent on CFO daily activities (from 1 to 4, where 1 is the most time-consuming and 4 is the least time-consuming)

Specification	Women		Men	
	Mean	*Median*	*Mean*	*Median*
Strategy development, general aims formulating, strategic thinking – Strategist	2.7	3	2.6	3
Strategic and operational communication across the company, internal team creating and working on diverse projects – Catalyst	2.9	3	2.9	3
Day-to-day financial management, financial department management – Operator	2.2	2	2.1	2
Financial planning and analysis, financial reporting to CEO – Steward	1.9	2	2.1	2

There is a similar number of male and female CFOs that have a financial stake in their current company, but for people having a stake in equity, men have twice a higher stake than women. This means that the source of power for women is their stake in the company.

Both women and men see raising capital and cash surplus management as the areas which they have the biggest impact. But women additionally also indicate the high impact on financial statement preparation (for men this activity was ranked at the level of 3).

The medium level of impact that male and female CFOs equally indicate is the creating strategy and long-term plans, investment decisions, and expenditures of the company's other departments. The lowest impact they perceive is in shaping the terms and conditions of paying for supplies and shaping the terms and conditions of getting payment from clients.

There are no significant differences in male and female CFOs' perception of impact on financial decisions.

Women and men perceive their responsibility in a similar way. They attribute the highest rank to raising capital and cash surplus management and financial statement preparation. They believe they are less responsible for creating strategy, investment decisions, and firm performance.

Female and male CFOs similarly ranked their daily activities. They spend most of the workday on financial planning and analysis, financial reporting to the CEO (Steward), day-to-day financial management, and financial department management (Operator). Focus on these two roles reflects the traditional approach to the CFO role and financial policy development. Less time is spent on a more modern perception of CFO role as Strategist (strategy development, general aims formulating, and strategic thinking) and Catalyst (strategic and operational communication across the company, internal team creating, and working on diverse projects).

4.1.2 Age and CFO risk attitude and CFO power

Since the literature documents that financial decisions depend on age (as younger present a more risky attitude), we ask questions if there are differences in terms of risk attitude provided to the company by younger and older CFOs.

Next, a couple of tables (Tables 4.9–4.16) reflect the CFOs' risk attitude both direct and indirect (overconfidence), and CFOs' age.

All answers "a" reflect a more risky attitude while "b" is less risky. There is no difference in risk attitude between older and middle-aged CFOs – they present a risky attitude in four cases out of seven. These four cases are common for all CFOs despite their age and they refer to the priority of real plans, timing for implementing profitable projects, minimizing cash pool, and minimizing inventories. Younger in five cases (out of seven) chose more risky answers. The younger CFOs are more risky when short-term financing is concerned.

There are more overconfident CFOs among younger CFOs (38%). The level of overconfidence decreases with age, among middle-aged CFOs, there are 31% of overconfident people, and among older CFOs, there are 21% of overconfident people.

Several next tables refer to the CFO power.

There are more younger CFOs (70%) that accept not to be a member of the board of directors. Among younger CFOs, there are 24% respondents who are a member of the board of directors. The older CFO is the more they are prone to be a member of the board of directors – among older CFOs, there are 36% of CFOs who are a member of the board of directors and 60% not being a member of the board of directors. This means that for older CFOs, the source of power is that they are a member of the board of directors.

Generally, there are no significant differences between subsamples in terms of the relationship between the CFO, the CEO, and the chief accounting officer. There are approximately 56% of cases in which the chief accounting officer reports to the CFO in every subsample.

There are more older CFOs (14%) than younger (10%) that have a stake in the company. However, the median stake for middle-aged CFOs is the highest (8%). This means that for older CFOs, the source of power is that they have a stake in the company's capital.

Raising capital, cash surplus management, and financial statement preparation are the areas that all subsamples think they have the biggest impact. The medium level of impact in all subsamples equally is pointed at creating strategy and expenditures of the company's other departments. Younger and middle-aged CFOs think they have quite a high impact on investment

Table 4.9 Distribution of the sample in terms of the CFO attitude towards financial decision

Specification	Up to 45 (n = 63)	from 46 to 55 (n = 64)	from 56 (n = 28)	Specification
1a) When creating plan, at the very beginning the investment spending is determined and then the capital should be found	More a (41, 65%)	More a (36, 56%)	More a (15, 54%)	1b) When creating plan, at the very beginning the available capital is determined and then the possible investment spending should be identified
2a) Every moment (even crisis) is good to implement profitable project no matter what the cash reserves are	More a (41, 65%)	More a (47, 73%)	More a (18, 64%)	2b) The profitable project should be implemented when having sufficient cash reserves and during economic boom
3a) When raising funds, the most important is to obtain them quickly no matter what is the cost of the funds	More b (35, 56%)	More b (41, 64%)	More b (19, 68%)	3b) When raising funds, the most important is to obtain them cheaply even if it takes more time
4a) Companies should use short-term financing (esp. trade credit)	More a (27, 43%)	More b (30, 47%)	More b (12, 43%)	4b) Companies should use long-term financing (esp. equity)
5a) The cash pool should be as low as possible due to its high opportunity cost	More a (27, 43%)	More a (27, 42%)	More a (14, 50%)	5b) The cash pool should be high due to future possible unpredictable events
6a) Companies should minimize the inventories due to their high maintenance costs	More a (37, 59%)	More a (41, 64%)	More a (19, 68%)	6b) Companies should have higher level of inventories in order to maintain the activity continuity
7a) When releasing voluntary disclosures, the company should publish information on specific events even if they are possible to occur	More b (51, 81%)	More b (46, 72%)	More b (25, 89%)	7b) When releasing voluntary disclosures, the company should publish information on specific events only after their occurrence

Table 4.10 Age and overconfidence

Specification	Up to 45		from 46 to 55		from 56	
	No.	%	No.	%	No.	%
Underconfidence	3	5	1	2	3	11
Confidence	36	57	43	67	19	68
Overconfidence	24	38	20	31	6	21

Table 4.11 Age and CFO membership in board of directors

Specification	Up to 45		From 46 to 55		From 56	
	No.	%	No.	%	No.	%
CFO not a member of a board	44	70	42	66	17	60
CFO a member of a board	15	24	15	23	10	36
CFO as a board member and another person as a director of financial department	4	6	7	11	1	4

Table 4.12 Age and distribution of the sample in terms of the person the chief accounting officer reports to

Specification	Up to 45		From 46 to 55		From 56	
	No.	%	No.	%	No.	%
Chief accounting officer reports to CFO	35	56	34	53	16	57
Chief accounting officer reports to CEO	21	33	28	44	11	39
Others	7	11	2	3	1	4

Table 4.13 Age and stake in the current company

Specification	Up to 45		From 46 to 55		From 56	
	No.	%	No.	%	No.	%
Yes	6	10	7	11	4	14
No	57	90	57	89	24	86
Median stake	2	x	8	x	4	x

Table 4.14 Age and distribution of the sample in terms of the perceived impact on the financial decisions (from 1 to 5, where 1 is the lowest impact and 5 is the biggest impact)

Specification	Up to 45		From 46 to 55		From 56	
	Mean	Median	Mean	Median	Mean	Median
Creating strategy and long-term plans	4.0	4	4.0	4	3.4	4
Investment decisions (in fixed assets: property, plant and equipment, mergers and acquisition)	3.7	4	3.8	4	3.2	3.5
Raising capital	4.5	5	4.6	5	4.3	5
Shaping the terms and conditions of paying for supplies	3.5	3	3.5	4	3.1	3
Shaping the terms and conditions of getting payment from clients	3.4	4	3.4	3	2.8	3
Cash surplus management	4.5	5	4.6	5	4.4	5
Expenditures of company's other departments	3.8	4	4.0	4	3.6	4
Choosing the methods of presentations of business activities in financial statement and timeliness of financial statement	4.5	5	4.6	5	4.3	5

Table 4.15 Age and distribution of the sample in terms of the perceived responsibilities for the results of the financial decisions (from 1 to 5, where 1 is the lowest responsibility and 5 is the biggest responsibility)

Specification	Up to 45		From 46 to 55		From 56	
	Mean	Median	Mean	Median	Mean	Median
Creating strategy and long-term plans	3.8	4	3.9	4	3.3	3.5
Investment decisions (in fixed assets: property, plant and equipment, mergers and acquisition)	3.6	4	3.6	4	3.1	3
Raising capital	4.4	5	4.6	5	4.2	5
Financial liquidity maintenance	4.6	5	4.6	5	4.5	5
Choosing the methods of presentations of business activities in financial statement and timeliness of financial statement	4.4	5	4.5	5	4.3	5
Financial firm performance and company's profitability	3.7	4	3.9	4	3.2	3

Table 4.16 Gender and distribution of the sample in terms of the time spent on CFO daily activities (from 1 to 4, where 1 is the most time-consuming and 4 is the least time-consuming)

Specification	Up to 45		From 46 to 55		From 56	
	Mean	Median	Mean	Median	Mean	Median
Strategy development, general aims formulating, strategic thinking – Strategist	2.6	3	2.6	3	2.8	3
Strategic and operational communication across the company, internal team creating and working on diverse projects – Catalyst	3.0	3	2.9	3	3.0	3
Day-to-day financial management, financial department management – Operator	2.0	2	2.3	2	1.8	1.5
Financial planning and analysis, financial reporting to CEO – Steward	2.0	2	2.0	2	2.0	1.5

decisions, and shaping the terms and conditions of paying for supplies and getting payment from clients (but not older CFOs).

CFOs from all subsamples similarly perceive their responsibility. All subsamples attribute the highest rank to raising capital and cash surplus management and financial statement preparation. However, older CFOs perceive that have lower than younger and middle-aged CFOs responsibility for creating strategy, investment decisions, and firm performance.

All CFOs from all subsamples perceive their activities in a similar way. They think that their duties focus on day-to-day financial management, financial department management (Operator), financial planning and analysis, and financial reporting to the CEO (Steward). However, older CFOs perceive their daily activities as Operator and Steward to a bigger extent than younger and middle aged. Less time is spent on the activities reflecting a more modern perception of CFOs roles Strategist (strategy development, general aims formulating, strategic thinking) and Catalyst (strategic and operational communication across the company, internal team creating and working on diverse projects).

4.2   CFO grouping and the risk attitude

We aimed to reveal specific characteristics of the CFO. But our sample turned out to be quite diversified. Thus we adopted the clustering method to present specific groups of CFOs.

Clustering algorithms exploit the underlying structure of the data distribution and define rules for grouping the data with similar characteristics. It is a method for finding cluster structure in a data set that is characterized by the greatest similarity within the same cluster and the greatest dissimilarity between different clusters.

We decided on the k-means clustering. K-means is one of the most popular unsupervised clustering algorithms for automatic data grouping into coherent clusters. This algorithm tries to group the data into K clusters by finding the cluster centroid (also known as cluster mean) and group with it the data points closest to it.

We decided to create four clusters, and adopt Ward linkage and Euclidean distance attitude. The number of clusters we choose (four) is optimal due to the size of the sample. The bigger number of clusters (even 5 or 6) might lead to small-size clusters or even zero-size clusters. Smaller number of clusters (2 or 3) might lead to grouping non-similar items. We use STATISTICA software to prepare clustering and dendrogram. To identify the clusters, we use several CFO characteristics such as the following: age, gender, educational background, previous experience, and stake in the current company. Table 4.17 presents characteristics of the CFOs' groups

The first cluster groups 32 CFOs. The dominant characteristics are as follows. These are mostly men, 46 years old and older, with strong experience in the CFO position (20 years and more) in many companies, not only the current company (2–4 companies). Apart from university education, they got MBA certificates and got education abroad. Additionally, they have foreign professional experience. Previously, they worked in financial institutions, and were members both in supervisory boards and the board of directors. That is why we coined the name for this group: forever directors.

The second cluster groups 53 CFOs. The dominant characteristics are as follows. These are mostly women, 46 years old and older, with slight experience in the CFO position (between 6–19 years) only in the current company. Apart from university education, they got an auditor certificate. They have no foreign experience (educational or professional). They have no previous experience which means that they have been working for the current company since the beginning. That is why we coined the name for this group: loyal accountant.

The third cluster groups 53 CFOs. The dominant characteristics are as follows. These are mostly men, between 30 and 45 years old, with slight experience in the CFO position (less than five years) only in the current company. Apart from university education, they got additional education such as postgraduate studies and they hold financial certificates. They have also some experience in studying abroad. They have previous experience as they worked in financial institutions, Big4, or audit companies. However, they have no experience in being a member of a supervisory board or board of directors. That is why we coined the name for this group: young and ambitious director.

Table 4.17 Characteristics of the CFOs' groups

Specification	Cluster 1: Male forever director/manager	Cluster 2: Loyal female accountant	Cluster 3: Young and ambitious male	Cluster 4: Female family member
N (number of people in the cluster)	32	53	53	17
Age	46–55	46–65	30–45	65 and more
Gender	Male	Female	Male	Female
Number of years of experience in the CFO position	More than 20 years	6–19 years	Less than 5	6–19 years
Number of companies that the position of CFO was hold	2–4	0	0	0
Additional courses	MBA certificate	Certified accountant/ auditor	Postgraduate studies and financial certificate	Lack
Foreign experience	Education and work	Lack	Education	Work
Previous professional experience	In financial institutions	Lack	In financial institutions, for audit company, or for big4,	Audit company
Member of board of directors	Yes, in a private and public company	No	No	No
Member of supervisory board	Yes, in a private and public company	No	No	Yes, in a private
Stake in the current company	No	No	No	Yes

The fourth cluster groups 17 CFOs. The dominant characteristics are as follows. These are mostly women, 46 years old and older, with slight experience in the CFO position (between 6 and19 years) only in the current company. They have no additional education. They have foreign experience in working abroad. They have also previous experience in audit companies. They have no experience in being a member of the board of directors. But they were members of supervisory board, probably in a company that is capitally linked to a current company. They also have some stake in the company which suggests that they are family members of the owners of the current company. That is why we coined the name for this group: female family members.

Next, several tables (Tables 4.18–4.22) present attitude towards CFOs' duties – their perception and time allocation.

Raising capital, cash surplus management, and financial statement preparation are the areas that all CFO clusters think they have the biggest impact. All subsamples equally point to the medium level of impact on creating strategy, investment decisions, and expenditures of the company's other departments.

But forever directors and female family members think they have a bigger impact on shaping the terms and conditions of paying for supplies.

Table 4.18 Clusters and distribution of the sample in terms of the perceived impact on the financial decisions (from 1 to 5, where 1 is the lowest impact and 5 is the biggest impact)

Specification	Cluster 1: Male forever directors	Cluster 2: loyal accountant	Cluster 3: young and ambitious director	Cluster 4: female family members
Creating strategy and long-term plans	4.3 (4)	3.6 (4)	3.0 (4)	3.9 (4)
Investment decisions (in fixed assets: property, plant and equipment, mergers and acquisition)	3.8 (4)	3.3 (4)	3.7 (4)	4.2 (4)
Raising capital	4.8 (5)	4.3 (5)	4.5 (5)	4.8 (5)
Shaping the terms and conditions of paying for supplies	3.6 (4)	3.3 (3)	3.4 (3)	3.8 (4)
Shaping the terms and conditions of getting payment from clients	3.3 (3)	3.1 (3)	3.4 (4)	3.8 (4)
Cash surplus management	4.8 (5)	4.4 (5)	4.3 (5)	4.8 (5)
Expenditures of company's other departments	3.9 (4)	3.9 (4)	3.8 (4)	3.9 (4)
Choosing the methods of presentations of business activities in financial statement and timeliness of financial statement	4.5 (5)	4.6 (5)	4.4 (5)	4.6 (5)

Note: Table presents mean and median (in parentheses) values.

Table 4.19 Clusters and distribution of the sample in terms of the perceived responsibilities for the results of the financial decisions (from 1 to 5, where 1 is the lowest responsibility and 5 is the biggest responsibility)

Specification	Cluster 1: Male forever directors	Cluster 2: loyal accountant	Cluster 3: young and ambitious director	Cluster 4: female family members
Creating strategy and long-term plans	4.0 (4)	3.5 (4)	3.8 (4)	3.9 (4)
Investment decisions (in fixed assets: property, plant and equipment, mergers and acquisition)	3.4 (4)	3.3 (3)	3.5 (4)	4.1 (4)
Raising capital	4.9 (5)	4.3 (5)	4.3 (5)	4.7 (5)
Financial liquidity maintenance	4.9 (5)	4.4 (5)	4.5 (5)	4.8 (5)
Choosing the methods of presentations of business activities in financial statement and timeliness of financial statement	4.6 (5)	4.4 (5)	4.3 (5)	4.6 (5)
Financial firm performance and company's profitability	3.8 (4)	3.5 (3)	3.8 (4)	4.1 (4)

Note: Table presents mean and median (in parentheses) values.

Table 4.20 Clusters and distribution of the sample in terms of the time spent on CFO daily activities (from 1 to 4, where 1 is the most time-consuming and 4 is the least time-consuming)

Specification	Cluster 1: Male forever directors	Cluster 2: loyal accountant	Cluster 3: young and ambitious director	Cluster 4: female family members
Strategy development, general aims formulating, strategic thinking – Strategist	2.5 (3)	2.8 (3)	2.6 (3)	2.4 (2)
Strategic and operational communication across the company, internal team creating and working on diverse projects – Catalyst	2.9 (3)	3.1 (3)	3.0 (3)	2.5 (3)
Day-to-day financial management, financial department management – Operator	2.3 (2)	2.0 (2)	2.1 (2)	2.2 (2)
Financial planning and analysis, financial reporting to CEO – Steward	2.0 (2)	1.9 (2)	2.0 (2)	2.3 (2)

Note: Table presents mean and median (in parentheses) values.

Table 4.21 CFOs clusters and distribution of the sample in terms of the CFO attitude towards risk of financial decision

Specification	Cluster 1 (n = 32) "Male forever director/manager"	Cluster 2 (n = 53) "Loyal female accountant"	Cluster 3 (n = 53) "Young and ambitious male"	Cluster 4 (n = 17) "Female family member"	Specification
1a) When creating plan, at the very beginning the investment spending is determined and then the capital should be found	More a (21, 66%)	More a (27, 51%)	More a (36, 68%)	More a (10, 59%)	1b) When creating plan, at the very beginning the available capital is determined and then the possible investment spending should be identified
2a) Every moment (even crisis) is good to implement profitable project no matter what the cash reserves are	More a (26, 81%)	More a (34, 64%)	More a (37, 70%)	More a (11, 65%)	2b) The profitable project should be implemented when having sufficient cash reserves and during economic boom
3a) When raising funds, the most important is to obtain them quickly no matter what is the cost of the funds	More b (23, 72%)	More b (33, 62%)	More b (34, 64%)	More b (7, 41%)	3b) When raising funds, the most important is to obtain them cheaply even if it takes more time
4a) Companies should use short-term financing (especially trade credit)	More a (16, 50%)	More a (23, 43%)	More b (21, 40%)	More b (9, 53%)	4b) Companies should use long-term financing (especially equity)
5a) The cash pool should be as low as possible due to its high opportunity cost	More a (14, 44%)	More a (25, 47%)	More a (22, 42%)	More b (8, 47%)	5b) The cash pool should be high due to future possible unpredictable events
6a) Companies should minimize the inventories due to their high maintenance costs	More a (25, 78%)	More a (32, 60%)	More a (31, 58%)	More a (9, 53%)	6b) Companies should have higher level of inventories in order to maintain the activity continuity
7a) When releasing voluntary disclosures, the company should publish information on specific events even if they are possible to occur	More b (26, 81%)	More b (44, 83%)	More b (39, 74%)	More b (13, 76%)	7b) When releasing voluntary disclosures, the company should publish information on specific events only after their occurrence

Table 4.22 CFOs' clusters and overconfidence

Specification	Cluster 1: Male forever directors		Cluster 2: loyal accountant		Cluster 3: young and ambitious director		Cluster 4: female family members	
	No.	%	No.	%	No.	%	No.	%
Underconfidence	1	3	3	6	2	4	1	6
Confidence	21	66	34	64	33	62	10	59
Overconfidence	10	31	16	30	18	34	6	35

Additionally, young and ambitious directors and female family members think they have a bigger impact on shaping the terms and conditions of getting payment from clients. The survey results show that loyal accountants perceive their impact on financial decisions as small.

CFOs from all clusters perceive their responsibility in a similar way. All subsamples attribute the highest rank to raising capital and cash surplus management and financial statement preparation. However, loyal accountants perceive that have lower responsibility for creating strategy, investment decisions, and firm performance.

Our survey reveals that female family members spend more time on Strategist duties than any other CFOs clusters. As for Steward, Operator, and Catalyst, all CFO clusters ranked them at similar levels.

All answers "a" reflect a more risky attitude while "b" is less risky. They present a risky attitude in five cases out of seven. The most risky attitude is presented by forever directors – in four cases out of seven (real over financial, investment timing, short-term financing, and inventory management). At the same time, they most conservative in two cases out of seven (raising capital and voluntary disclosure). It seems that they are the most radical in their attitudes.

Loyal accountant is also risky in five cases out of seven, but they show a high level of risky attitude only in two cases (cash and inventory management). They show a conservative attitude in two cases out of seven but only in one high level of conservativeness (voluntary disclosure).

Young and ambitious directors show a risky attitude in four cases out of seven being the most risky in two cases (real over financial, and investment timing). They show a conservative attitude in three out of seven cases with one being the most conservative (raising capital).

Female family members show risky attitude in three cases out of seven, but their level of riskiness is moderate. They show a conservative attitude in four cases out of seven with two very conservative (short-term financing and cash management).

There are more underconfident CFOs among loyal accountant and female family members. But there are more overconfident CFOs among forever directors, young and ambitious directors, and female family members.

4.3   Indexing the risk attitude and CFO power

Apart from grouping our sample CFOs, we developed several indexes describing risk attitude and CFO power. As for risk attitude, we developed three indexes:

- index of direct measure (DIRECT_INDEX);
- index of indirect measure (INDIRECT_INDEX);
- the overconfidence index (OC_INDEX).

As for CFO power, we develop one index (POWER_INDEX)

Direct measure of risk attitude is based on Graham et al. (2013) attitude. Following Graham et al. (2013), we attempt to identify personal risk-aversion by asking questions on the CFO's attitude towards financial issues such as planning, investment decisions, financing, cash holdings, inventory management, and voluntary disclosures. We ask sample CFOs to follow their own feelings not connected with the actual situation of the company they work for. We ask the CFO to choose one out of two options. If they choose more "b" answers they reflect a more risk-averse attitude. For each "b" answer, we appoint 1 point and 0 otherwise. Then, we divided the collected points by seven as we have seven areas in this question. As a result, we got the value of risk attitude in the range 0 and 1; if there are more risky answers (b) then the direct index is close to 1, and if there are more safe answers (a) then the direct index is close to 0.

Indirect measure (INDIRECT_INDEX) includes gender, age, education (additional and abroad), and experience (as a board member, foreign experience, number of years in the position of CFO in general, and a number of companies they were in the CFO positions) areas.

As for gender, we appoint 1 if a man is in the position of CFO and 0 otherwise. This is justified by the notion that men are supposed to be more risky.

As for age, we appoint three points: 1, 2, or 3 depending on the age. If the CFO is older than 55 we appoint 1 point, if CFO is between 46 and 55, we appoint 2 points, and if the CFO is younger than 45, we appoint 3 points. Then, we divided the appointed points by three to get the value in the range between 0 and 1. The justification of appointing 1 point to older CFOs and 3 to younger CFOs is justified by the fact that younger people take more risky actions and have a more risky attitude and in the results they will be closer to 1. Older people take less risky actions and have less risky attitude and in the results, they will be closer to 0.

As for additional education, we appoint 1 point if CFOs have no additional education (courses, postgraduate studies, and certificates) and 0 if there is at least one additional education.

As for education abroad, we appoint 1 point if CFOs have no education abroad and 0 if there is any education abroad. The justification for appointing

0 points for having additional education or education abroad lies in the assumption that educated people have less risky attitude. There is some research showing that a professional education in management, i.e. the executive manager has a post-degree specialization such as an MBA or a PhD, is associated with risk aversion, since such executives are primarily trained to avoid big losses and mistakes. Orens and Reheul (2013) concur by suggesting that more educated managers tend to pursue long-term development and do not invest in higher-variance projects, which can generate big losses. (Martino et al., 2020)

As for experience as a board member (board of directors or supervisory board – in a private or public company) we appoint 1 if CFO has any experience as a board member and 0 otherwise.

As for foreign experience, we appoint 1 if CFO has any foreign experience and 0 otherwise.

As for a number of years they are in the position of CFO not only in the current company but in general we appoint points depending on the number of years. If CFO has experience shorter than five years in the position of CFO then we appoint 4 points; if CFO has the experience between 6 and 10 years we appoint 3 points; if CFO has the experience between 11 and 20 years we appoint 2 points; if CFO has the experience longer than 20 years, we appoint 1 point. Then, we divided the appointed points by four to get the value in the range between 0 and 1.

As for a number of companies (except the current company) that were in the CFO positions we took into account the number of these companies and divided it by 6 (because a maximum number of companies the surveyed CFOs worked for) to get the value in the range between 0 and 1. The justification for such an attitude is that we believe that the better the experience the higher risk attitude. Farag and Mallin (2016) provide empirical support for this argument, finding a positive and highly significant relationship between CEO's previous board experience and corporate risk-taking. They argue that CEOs with professional experience outside the company are more innovative and demonstrate higher openness to and awareness of new opportunities (Orens and Reheul 2013); thus, they are more risk-willing than CEOs with experience in the same company (Martino et al., 2020).

To calculate the Indirect measure of risk attitude, we add up all these eight partial points, with all of them being in the range between 0 and 1: gender, age additional education, education abroad, experience as a board member, foreign experience, number of years in the position of CFO in general, and a number of companies they were in the CFO position. The sum was later divided by 8 (as there are eight parts of indirect measure) to get the value in the range between 0 and 1, when more risky is closer to 1, and less risky is closer to 0. Figure 4.1 shows the components of INDIRECT_INDEX.

We perceive overconfidence as a separate indirect measure of risk attitude and an alternative measure to this indirect presented above. It includes three components: estimation of own knowledge, placement of success and failure,

INDIRECT MEASURE OF RISK ATTITUDE (INDIRECT_INDEX)				
		RISK-AVERSE (0)		RISK-TAKING (1)
GENDER (GEN)		Woman		Man
AGE (AGE)		≥56	46–55	≤45
EDUCATION	Additional (ADD_EDU)	Yes		No
	Abroad (EDU_ABR)	Yes		No
EXPERIENCE	Board member (EXP_BOARD)	No		Yes
	Foreign experience (EXP_ABR)	No		Yes
	Number of years as CFO (CFO_TENURE)	≥20 11–19	6–10	≤5
	Number of companies as CFO (CFO_NO_FIRMS)	1 2 3	4	5 ≥6

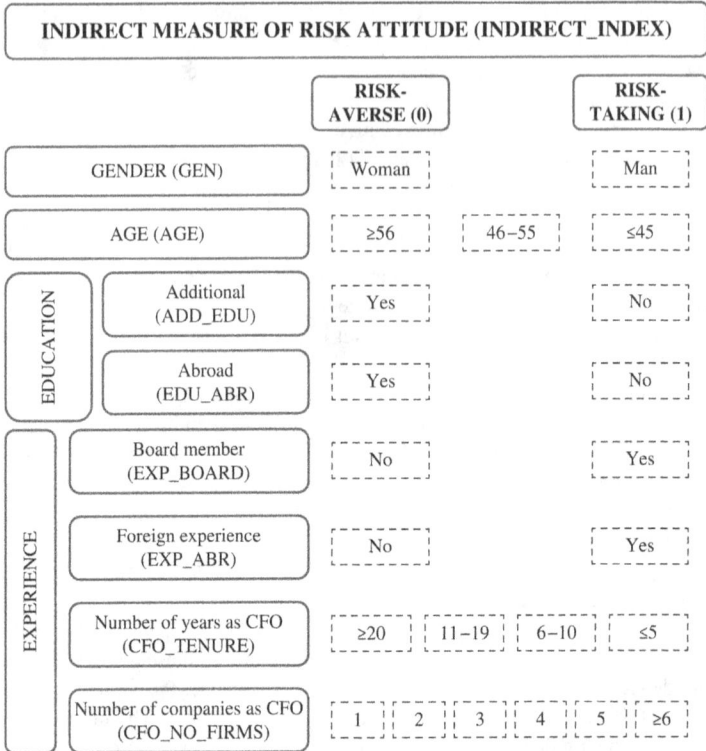

Figure 4.1 The components of INDIRECT_INDEX

and attitude towards others and future. The methodology of overconfidence identification was provided in Chapter 3. Initially, we got the value 1 if underconfident, 2 if confident, and 3 if overconfident. We divided it by 3 to get the value in the range between 0 and 1, when more risky is closer to 1, and less risky is closer to 0. The justification is the fact that overconfident people cannot see the risk and thus they usually take more risky activities (Graham et al., 2013; Wrońska-Bukalska, 2016; Bukalska, 2020). Figure 4.2 shows the components of the overconfidence index (OC_INDEX).

The last index reflects CFO power. It consists of several aspects: the number of years of work for the current company, the share of the current company capital the CFO and their families hold, the CFO's position in the company structure (especially whether the CFO is a member of the board of directors), and who the chief accounting officer reports to (directly to CEO, directly to CFO).

THE LEVEL OF CONFIDENCE (OC_INDEX)	
UNDERCONFIDENCE (0)	**OVERCONFIDENCE (1)**
ESTIMATION	Underestimation	Overestimation
PLACEMENT	Underplacement	Overplacement
OPTIMISM vs. PESIMISM	Pesimism	Optimism

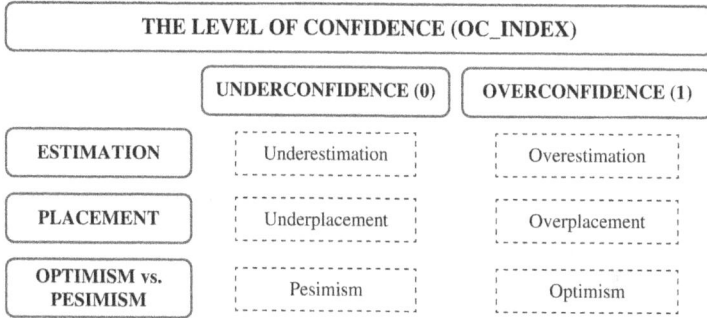

Figure 4.2 The components of OC_INDEX

As for the number of years of work for the current company, we appoint three points depending on the number of years, 1 point if the CFO works shorter than 10 years, 2 points if the CFO works between 10 and 19 years, and 3 points if the CFO works longer than 20 years. Then, we divided it by 3 to get the value in the range between 0 and 1, when more powerful is closer to 1, and less powerful is closer to 0. We believe that a person is more powerful if the CFO works longer for the company.

As for the the share of the current company capital the CFO and their families hold, we implement a dummy variable: 1 if the CFO has any stake in the company, and 0 otherwise. We believe that a person is more powerful if the CFO has stake in the company.

As for the CFO position in the company structure, we take into account whether the CFO is a member of the board of directors. Again, we implemented a dummy variable: 1 if the CFO is a member of the board of directors, and 0 otherwise. We believe that a person is more powerful if CFO is a member of the board of directors.

As for who the chief accounting officer reports to: directly to the CEO or directly to the CFO, we implemented a dummy variable: 1 if the chief accounting officer reports directly to CFO, and 0 otherwise. We believe that person is more powerful if the chief accounting officer reports directly to the CFO.

To calculate the POWER_INDEX, we add up all these four partial points, with all of them being in the range between 0 and 1: number of years of work for the current company, the share of the current company capital the CFO and their families hold, the CFO position in the company structure (especially whether the CFO is a member of board of directors), and who the chief accounting officer report to (directly to CEO, directly to CFO). The sum was later divided by 4 (as there are four parts of the power index) to get the value in the range between 0 and 1, when more powerful is closer to 1, and less powerful is closer to 0. The components of the CFO power index are presented in Figure 4.3.

CFO POWER (POWER_INDEX)		
	LESS POWERFUL (0)	**MORE POWERFUL** (1)
Number of years for current company (FIRM_TENURE)	0–9 10–19	≥20
CFO's stake in the company (CFO_STAKE)	No	Yes
CFO as a board member (CFO_BOARD)	No	Yes
Who the CAO reports to (CFO_CAO)?	Other person than CFO	CFO

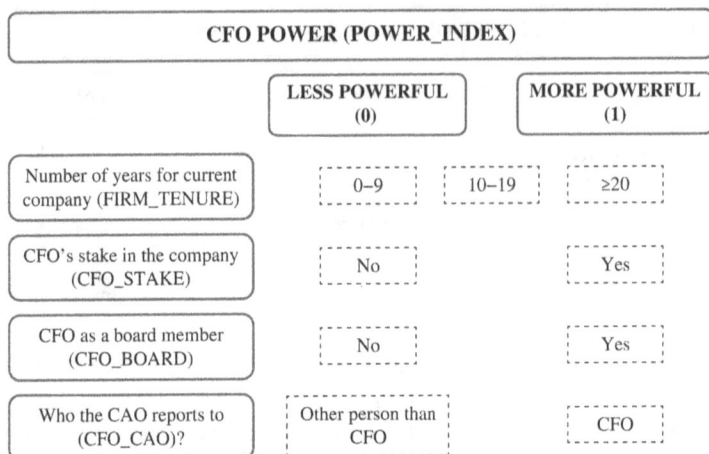

Figure 4.3 The components of CFO POWER_INDEX

Table 4.23 presents the descriptive statistics of risk and power indexes.

All indexes are in the range between 0 and 1, where 1 reflects a highly risky attitude and high power. But the direct and indirect measures of risk attitude show that surveyed CFOs present relatively low level of riskiness, as the mean and median are lower than 0.5. The same is true with power index – surveyed CFOs have low power in their companies – the power index is lower than 0.5 (mean and median). But our surveyed CFOs show a high level of overconfidence with a mean of 0.74 and median of 0.67.

Additionally, we calculate the correlation coefficients between the index value for each surveyed CFO and their perception of impact and responsibilities but also their daily duties. We implemented Spearman correlation as we dealt with ordinal variables. The correlation matrixes are presented in Tables 4.24–4.26.

The higher the direct measure of risk attitude, the higher the perceived impact on only cash management is. The higher the indirect measure of risk attitude, the higher the perceived impact on creating strategy and cash management. The

Table 4.23 Descriptive statistics of risk and power indexes

Specification	DIRECT	INDIRECT	OC	POWER
Mean	0.4560	0.4633	0.7407	0.4032
Median	0.4286	0.4479	0.6667	0.3333
Maximum	0.8571	0.8854	1.0000	1.0000
Minimum	0.0000	0.1979	0.3333	0.0833
Std. Dev.	0.2288	0.1371	0.1871	0.2283

Table 4.24 Correlation matrix between indexes and CFO's perceived impact on the financial decisions (from 1 to 5, where 1 is the lowest impact and 5 is the biggest impact)

Specification	DIRECT	INDIRECT	OC	POWER
Creating strategy and long-term plans	0.103	0.227**	0.190*	0.214**
Investment decisions (in fixed assets: property, plant and equipment, mergers and acquisition)	−0.035	0.078	−0.097	0.223***
Raising capital	0.034	0.089	−0.106	0.253**
Shaping the terms and conditions of paying for supplies	−0.137	−0.003	0.180*	0.021
Shaping the terms and conditions of getting payment from clients	−0.088	0.009	0.100	0.199*
Cash surplus management	0.168*	0.168*	0.072	0.210**
Expenditures of company's other departments	−0.061	0.037	0.023	0.122
Choosing the methods of presentations of business activities in financial statements and timeliness of financial statement	−0.026	0.051	−0.014	0.138

Note: *, **, and *** indicate significance at the 10%, 5%, and 1% levels, respectively.

higher the overconfidence the higher, the perceived impact on creating strategy and shaping the terms and conditions of paying for supplies. This means that CFOs with the highest risk attitude perceive their impact as quite low.

But the higher the power index the higher the perceived impact on creating strategy, investment decisions, raising capital, shaping the terms and conditions of getting payment from clients, and cash management. This means that

Table 4.25 Correlation matrix between indexes and CFO's perceived responsibilities for the results of the financial decisions (from 1 to 5, where 1 is the lowest responsibility and 5 is the biggest responsibility)

Specification	DIRECT	INDIRECT	OC	POWER
Creating strategy and long-term plans	0.214**	0.087	0.043	0.155
Investment decisions (in fixed assets: property, plant and equipment, mergers and acquisition)	−0.017	−0.026	−0.014	0.244**
Raising capital	0.078	0.164	0.055	0.216**
Financial liquidity maintenance	0.017	0.155	0.129	0.250**
Choosing the methods of presentations of business activities in financial statement and timeliness of financial statement	0.009	0.152	0.003	0.212**
Financial firm performance and company's profitability	−0.118	0.072	0.066	0.123

Note: *, **, and *** indicate significance at the 10%, 5%, and 1% levels, respectively.

Table 4.26 Correlation matrix between indexes and CFO's time spent on CFO daily activities (from 1 to 4, where 1 is the most time-consuming and 4 is the least time-consuming)

Specification	DIRECT	INDIRECT	OC	POWER
Strategy development, general aims formulating, strategic thinking – Strategist	−0.170*	−0.015	−0.106	0.127
Strategic and operational communication across the company, internal team creating and working on diverse projects – Catalyst	−0.037	−0.295***	−0.144	−0.116
Day-to-day financial management, financial department management – Operator	0.116	−0.047	0.064	−0.005
Financial planning and analysis, financial reporting to CEO – Steward	0.035	0.141	0.097	−0.127

Note: *, **, and *** indicate significance at the 10%, 5%, and 1% levels, respectively.

the power is quite a strong factor affecting the perception of the impact on financial decisions.

It seems that CFOs with higher risk attitude (both direct and indirect, and connected with overconfidence) perceive their responsibilities at a low level. Only a high level of direct index is connected with a high perception of responsibility for strategy creation. The higher the power index, the higher the perception of responsibility for investment decisions, raising capital, financial liquidity maintenance, and financial statements. And again, this means that the power is quite a strong factor affecting the perception of the responsibility for financial decisions.

It seems that CFOs' risk attitude and power have no impact on daily activities. But there are two exceptions: the higher direct and indirect index of risk attitude the most time-consuming activities are those connected with Strategist and Catalyst, respectively.

To sum up, it seems that CFOs' power is more important in determining their perception of impact and responsibilities for financial decisions. The bigger CFOs' power the CFOs' perception of their impact is higher. Additionally, the higher the risk attitude (indirect and overconfidence) the bigger the perceived impact on creating strategy. As for CFOs' daily duties, it seems that higher the direct measure of their risk attitude the more time-consuming activities are those connected with Strategist activities.

***

We find that surveyed CFOs differ in terms of their demographic characteristics. We also find that demographic characteristics are important for their way to get the CFO position. Women in the position of CFO are generally older which indicates that they enter the CFO position later. Men enter the CFO position earlier after a shorter period of work for the company. Additionally, women and older CFOs have more traditional additional education than men and younger CFOs. As for attitude towards financial decisions, women are riskier – they show a risky attitude in more issues and their riskiness is higher. The main source of power for men is being a member of the board of directors and their position in the company's structure while the main source of power for women is their stake in the company. Men and women perceive in a similar way their impact and responsibility for financial making decisions

There is quite a big difference between older and younger CFOs. But there are strong similarities between younger and middle CFOs. We believe that in 1989 middle-aged CFOs finished their studies and started their professional career in new economic conditions. There is no difference in risk attitude between older and middle-aged CFOs. Younger CFOs in five cases (out of seven) chose more risky answers but their riskiness is moderate. There are more overconfident CFOs among younger CFOs (38%). The level of overconfidence decreases with age, as among middle-aged CFOs, there are 31% of overconfident people, and among older CFOs there 21% overconfident people. There are no significant differences in the perception of the impact and responsibilities of financial decisions. They think that their duties focus on day-to-day financial management, financial department management (Operator) and financial planning and analysis, financial reporting to the CEO (Steward).

We identify four clusters taking into account age, gender, some of the CFOs' experience variables, and some of the CFOs' power variables. As a result, we were able to develop four clusters of CFOs: Cluster 1 – forever directors, Cluster 2 – loyal accountant; Cluster 3 – young and ambitious directors, and Cluster 4 – female family members. We find that raising capital, cash surplus management, and financial statement preparation are the areas that all CFO clusters think they have the biggest impact. But forever directors and female family members think they have a bigger impact on shaping the terms and conditions of paying for supplies. The survey results show that loyal accountants perceive their impact on financial decisions as small.

CFOs from all clusters perceive their responsibility in a similar way. Our survey reveals that female family members spend more time on Strategist duties than any other CFOs clusters. As for Steward, Operator, and Catalyst, all CFO clusters ranked them at similar levels. The most risky attitude is presented by forever directors, then young and ambitious directors while female family members show a less risky attitude. There are more overconfident CFOs among forever directors, young and ambitious directors, and female family members.

Additionally, we develop risk attitude and power indexes that are taken into account when trying to find out the impact of CFOs on financial decisions and firm performance. It turns out that it is not their risk attitude that is important for their perception of the impact and responsibilities but their power.

5 CFO characteristics and corporate financial decisions

5.1 Methodology and descriptive statistics

Further research is devoted to unveiling the role of the CFO in financial decision-making. The role of the CFO is depicted by four indexes: DIRECT, INDIRECT, OC, and POWER. Additionally, the picture of the CFO is developed with four groups of CFOs (male forever director, loyal female accountant, young and ambitious male, and female family member). Financial decisions are depicted by debt ratio and cash ratio. Firm financial performance is depicted by profitability (ROA). Additionally, we included variable COVID-19 trying to find out the impact of the crisis on the role and the impact of the CFO. We were able to collect the financial data for 99 companies out of 155 surveyed, thus the following analysis is limited to those 99. Financial data covers the years before the COVID-19 crisis: 2017–2019 and during the COVID-19 crisis: 2020.

Table 5.1 presents the definition of variables included in the research

Those variables were later employed to find the relationship between CFOs' characteristics and financial variables. Therefore, firstly we conducted a comparative analysis to find out if there are differences between the four groups of companies managed by different CFOs (Section 5.2). Secondly, we build the regression models with financial variables as dependent variables: TOTLIAB_ASSET, CASH_ASSET, and ROA to detect if financial decisions and the firm's performance are affected by the CFO's demographic characteristics and CFO power (Section 5.3). Generally, according to our hypotheses, we assume that the higher risk attitude (measured in direct and indirect ways) the higher financial leverage (TOTLIAB_ASSET), the lower cash holdings (CASH_ASSET), and higher firm performance (ROA).

Table 5.2 presents basic descriptive statistics of variables included in the research.

Our research plan covers finding the differences between the groups (identified in Section 4.2: male forever director, loyal female accountant, young and ambitious male, and female family member) and then modelling the impact of CFO attitude towards risk and CFO power on financial decisions and firm performance with the indexes implemented.

DOI: 10.4324/9781003473190-6

Table 5.1 The definition of variables included in the research

Variable	Definition	Value
Panel A: Aggregated measures of CFO's characteristics		
DIRECT_INDEX	Direct index – the measure of CFO's risk attitude that is based on survey questionnaire answers	In the range between 0 and 1, where 1 reflects more risky attitude
INDIRECT_INDEX	Indirect index – the measure of CFO's risk attitude that is based on demographic characteristics	In the range between 0 and 1, where 1 reflects more risky attitude
OC_INDEX	Overconfidence index – the measure of CFO's overconfidence that is based on survey questionnaire answers	In the range between 0 and 1, where 1 reflects overconfidence (more risky attitude)
POWER_INDEX	Power index that reflects the CFO's power	In the range between 0 and 1, where 1 reflects more powerful CFO
Panel B: INDIRECT INDEX components		
GEN	Gender	Dummy variable: 1 for men, 0 otherwise
AGE	Age	In the range between 0 and 1, where 1 reflects more risky (younger) CFO
ADD_EDU	Additional education	Dummy variable: 1 for no additional education, 0 otherwise
EDU_ABR	Education abroad	Dummy variable: 1 for no education abroad, 0 otherwise
EXP_BOARD	Experience as a board member	Dummy variable: 1 for having any board experience, 0 otherwise
EXP_ABR	Foreign experience	Dummy variable: 1 for having any experience abroad, 0 otherwise
EXP_TENURE	Number of years in the position of CFO in general	In the range between 0 and 1, where 1 reflects more risky (fewer years in the position) CFO
EXP_NOFIRM	Number of companies they were in the CFO position	In the range between 0 and 1, where 1 reflects more risky (more companies) CFO

(Continued)

Table 5.1 (Continued)

Variable	Definition	Value
Panel C: POWER_INDEX components		
FIRM_TENURE	Number of years of work for the current company	In the range between 0 and 1, where 1 reflects more powerful (more years of work for the current company) CFO
CFO_STAKE	The share of the current company capital the CFO and their families hold	Dummy variable: 1 if CFO has any stake in the company, and 0 otherwise
CFO_BOARD	The CFO position in the company structure (especially whether the CFO is a member of the board of directors	Dummy variable: 1 if CFO is a member of the board of directors, and 0 otherwise
CFO_CAO	Who the chief accounting officer reports to (directly to CEO or directly to CFO)	Dummy variable: 1 if the chief accounting officer reports directly to CFO, and 0 otherwise
Panel D: Financial variables		
ROA	Firm performance – return on assets which is calculated as net profit divided by total assets	%
TOTLIAB_ASSET	Financing decisions – debt ratio which is calculated as total liabilities to total assets	%
CASH_ASSET	Financial liquidity – cash ratio which is calculated as cash to total assets	%
TAT	Asset turnover ratio which is calculated as total sales to average assets	
CURRENT_RATIO	Current ratio of financial liquidity which is calculated as current assets to current liabilities	
GROWTH	sales growth ratio	%
TOTASS	Size – total assets	Thousand of PLN
LN_TOTASS	Size – natural logarithm of total assets	

Table 5.2 Descriptive statistics of the sample

Variables	Mean	Median	Maximum	Minimum	Std. Dev.	n
Panel A: Aggregated measures of CFO's characteristics						
DIRECT_INDEX	0.4560	0.4286	0.8571	0.0000	0.2288	396
INDIRECT_INDEX	0.4633	0.4479	0.8854	0.1979	0.1371	396
OC_INDEX	0.7407	0.6667	1.0000	0.3333	0.1871	396
POWER_INDEX	0.4032	0.3333	1.0000	0.0833	0.2283	396
Panel B: INDIRECT INDEX components						
GEN	0.5051	1.0000	1.0000	0.0000	0.5006	396
AGE	0.7138	0.6667	1.0000	0.3333	0.2465	396
ADD_EDU	0.1919	0.0000	1.0000	0.0000	0.3943	396
EDU_ABR	0.7980	1.0000	1.0000	0.0000	0.4020	396
EXP_BOARD	0.4747	0.0000	2.0000	0.0000	0.6876	396
EXP_ABR	0.1616	0.0000	1.0000	0.0000	0.3686	396
EXP_TENURE	0.6591	0.7500	1.0000	0.2500	0.2649	396
EXP_NOFIRM	0.2020	0.1667	1.0000	0.0000	0.2291	396
Panel C: POWER_INDEX components						
FIRM_TENURE	0.5926	0.6667	1.0000	0.3333	0.2490	396
CFO_STAKE	0.1414	0.0000	1.0000	0.0000	0.3489	396
CFO_BOARD	0.3232	0.0000	1.0000	0.0000	0.4683	396
CFO_CAO	0.5556	1.0000	1.0000	0.0000	0.4975	396
Panel D: Financial variables						
ROA	0.0464	0.0446	0.7466	−2.0035	0.1567	395
TAT	1.6829	1.4613	7.7605	0.0278	1.2524	297
TOTLIAB_ASSET	0.5094	0.4905	2.4250	0.0080	0.2623	395
CASH_ASSET	0.0982	0.0406	0.7995	0.0000	0.1249	395
CURRENT_RATIO	2.6213	1.5043	112.2984	0.2144	8.0409	395
GROWTH	0.1025	0.0370	5.2877	−0.9236	0.4764	295
TOTASS	226549	98,657	3,316,565	0.001	396434	396

To identify the differences between groups, we implement ANOVA (analysis of variance) F-test for equality of means and median chi-square test. Using these tests, we try to find out whether there are any differences in financial corporate strategy between the groups (identified in Section 4.1: male forever director, loyal female accountant, young and ambitious male, and female family member).

To model the impact of CFO characteristics on financial data, we applied OLS regression analysis. Because our financial data covers two subperiods, we include a dummy variable describing the impact of the COVID-19 crisis (0 – non-crisis, 1 – COVID-19 crisis year). Additionally, we included interactive variables to find the connected impact of the CFO during the COVID-19 crisis.

Generally, we calculate the impact of risk attitude and power (represented by indexes) on financial decisions and firm performance, but we also calculate the impact of elements included in the index (e.g. age, gender, etc.). But in tables, we present the impact of indexes on financial decisions no matter whether it is statistically significant or not. However, we present the impact of elements included in the indexes only if we find they are statistically significant. In tables with regression analysis results, we present the beta coefficient, t-statistics, and p-value presented by asterisks.

5.2   Group comparative analysis

To identify the differences between groups, we implement ANOVA (analysis of variance) F-test for equality of means and median chi-square test. Using these tests, we try to find out whether there are any differences in financial corporate strategy between the groups (identified in Section 4.1: 1) male forever director, 2) loyal female accountant, 3) young and ambitious male, and 4) female family member).

Table 5.3 presents the results of testing the differences between the groups of CFOs in terms of total assets.

We find that the companies with different types of CFOs differ with a statistical significance both in terms of the mean and median value of total assets. Male forever directors and young and ambitious males work for bigger companies, while loyal female accountants and female family members work for smaller companies.

Table 5.4 presents the results of testing the differences between the groups of CFOs in terms of sales growth ratio.

We find that the companies with different types of CFOs do not differ with a statistical significance both in terms of mean and median growth rate. The average growth rate is 10% and the median is 4%.

Table 5.3 Results of testing the differences between the groups of CFOs in terms of total assets

Descriptive statistics					Statistical significance of distance	
Group	Mean	Std. Dev.	Median	n	Method	Value
1 male forever director	293,773	368,849	40,245	84	Anova F-test	2.2929
2 loyal female accountant	175,194	195,183	16,265	144	probability	0.0776*
3 young and ambitious male	266,484	614,902	58,103	112	Med. Chi-square	8.9325
4 female family member	177,898	204,409	27,315	56	probability	0.0302**
All	226,549	396,434	19,922	396		

Note: *, **, and *** indicate significance at the 10%, 5%, and 1% levels, respectively.

Table 5.4 Results of testing the differences between the groups of CFOs in terms of growth

Descriptive statistics					Statistical significance of distance	
Group	Mean	Std. Dev.	Median	n	Method	Value
1 male forever director	0.0689	0.4049	0.0113	63	Anova F-test	0.5580
2 loyal female accountant	0.1500	0.6405	0.0495	106	probability	0.6432
3 young and ambitious male	0.0756	0.3614	0.0351	84	Med. Chi-square	3.1476
4 female family member	0.0869	0.2344	0.0667	42		
All	0.1025	0.4764	0.0370	295	probability	0.3694

Note: ˙, ˙˙, and ˙˙˙ indicate significance at the 10%, 5%, and 1% levels, respectively.

Table 5.5 presents the results of the comparison of the debt ratio for CFO groups

We find that the companies with different types of CFOs do not differ with a statistical significance. The average debt ratio (mean relation of total liabilities to total assets) stands at 50%. But while digging deeper, we find that half of the companies with CFOs being loyal female accountants or young and ambitious males have lower debt ratios (due to low median of debt ratio).

Table 5.6 presents the results of the comparison of the cash ratio for groups.

We find that the companies with different types of CFOs differ with a statistical significance. The average cash ratio (mean relation of cash holdings to total assets) stands at 10%. The mean cash ratio for companies with

Table 5.5 Comparison of the debt ratio for CFO groups

Descriptive statistics					Statistical significance of distance	
Group	Mean	Std. Dev.	Median	n	Method	Value
1 male forever director	0.5439	0.2282	0.5431	84	Anova F-test	0.6530
2 loyal female accountant	0.5005	0.2718	0.4407	143	probability	0.5815
3 young and ambitious male	0.5049	0.2866	0.4779	112	Med. Chi-square	6.8077
4 female family member	0.4897	0.2357	0.5165	56		
All	0.5094	0.2623	0.4905	395	probability	0.0783˙

Note: ˙, ˙˙, and ˙˙˙ indicate significance at the 10%, 5%, and 1% levels, respectively.

Table 5.6 Comparison of the cash ratio for groups

Descriptive statistics					Statistical significance of distance	
Group	Mean	Std. Dev.	Median	n	Method	Value
1 male forever director	0.0424	0.0528	0.0291	84	Anova F-test	11.0384
2 loyal female accountant	0.0904	0.1246	0.0304	143	probability	0.0000***
3 young and ambitious male	0.1378	0.1271	0.1030	112	Med. Chi-square	24.1054
4 female family member	0.1228	0.1617	0.0502	56		
All	0.0982	0.1249	0.0406	395	probability	0.0000***

Note: *, **, and *** indicate significance at the 10%, 5%, and 1% levels, respectively.

male forever directors is the lowest, then loyal female accountants, and female family members, and the highest is for companies with young and ambitious males. Similar results are obtained when comparing the median cash ratio: a lower cash ratio is present in companies with a male forever director and loyal female accountant, and a higher median cash ratio is present in companies with female family members and young and ambitious males.

Table 5.7 presents the results of a comparison of the profitability (ROA) for groups.

We find that the companies with different types of CFOs differ with a statistical significance both in terms of mean and median profitability. The average profitability is 5%. The profitability is lower for companies with male

Table 5.7 Comparison of the profitability (ROA) for groups

Descriptive statistics					Statistical significance of distance	
Group	Mean	Std. Dev.	Median	n	Method	Value
1 male forever director	0.0233	0.0805	0.0385	84	Anova F-test	2.3392
2 loyal female accountant	0.0340	0.1131	0.0381	143	probability	0.0730*
3 young and ambitious male	0.0606	0.2363	0.0636	112	Med. Chi-square	7.5814
4 female family member	0.0845	0.1315	0.0611	56		
All	0.0464	0.1567	0.0446	395	probability	0.0555*

Note: *, **, and *** indicate significance at the 10%, 5%, and 1% levels, respectively.

forever directors and loyal female accountants, while it is higher for companies with female family members and young and ambitious males.

To sum up, a male forever director works for a bigger company, with lower growth, a higher debt ratio, lower cash holdings, and lower profitability. Similarly, a young and ambitious male works for a bigger company, with low growth, lower debt ratio, high cash holdings, and higher profitability. A loyal female accountant works for a small company, with quite high growth, a lower debt ratio and cash ratio, and low profitability. And female family member works for a small company with quite high growth, with a lower debt ratio, high cash ratio, and higher profitability. Our results confirm the assumption that the CFO's demographic characteristics might be important for financial decisions and financial performance.

5.3 Regression analysis results

To model the impact of CFO characteristics on financial data, we applied OLS regression analysis. Because our financial data covers two subperiods we include a dummy variable describing the impact of the COVID-19 crisis (0 for non-crisis years, 1 for COVID-19 crisis year). Additionally, we included interactive variables to find the connected impact of the CFO during the COVID-19 crisis.

Generally, we calculate the impact of risk attitude and power (represented by indexes) on financial decisions and firm performance, but we also calculate the impact of elements included in the index (e.g. age, gender, etc.). But in tables, we present the impact of indexes on financial decisions no matter whether it is statistically significant or not. We present the impact of elements included in the indexes only if we find they are statistically significant.

In tables with regression analysis results, we present the beta coefficient, and t-statistics, and the p-value is represented by asterisks. Firstly, we conducted a regression analysis to detect if CFO's characteristics affect the level of indebtedness (see Table 5.8).

All models are statistically significant (F-statistics) with R-squared higher than 0.30 which means that all variables included in the model explain 30% of the variability of the dependent variable.

However, we find that only the DIRECT_INDEX of risk attitude is statistically significant, but it negatively impacts the debt ratio. This means that the higher the DIRECT_INDEX (more risky attitude), the lower the debt ratio is. One would expect that the CFO's propensity to take risks would result in higher indebtedness. But we received the opposite results. There are at least two possible explanations for that. Firstly, indebtedness might not be considered as a source of financial risk and failure. This statement was confirmed by the research for SMEs in the Czech Republic that provides evidence that debt is perceived by executives as an insignificant factor of failure (Kramoliš and Dobeš, 2020). Secondly, the CFO's individual risk attitude might be

Table 5.8 Regression analysis results with debt ratio (TOTLIAB_ASSET) as the dependent variable

Variable	1	2	3	4	5	6
C	0.3908***	0.4694***	0.4235***	0.4090***	0.3694***	0.4521***
COVID	0.0704	-0.0177	0.0153	0.0447	0.0833	0.0576
INDIRECT_INDEX	0.0866					
INDIRECT_INDEX*COVID	-0.1419					
DIRECT_INDEX		-0.1594**				
DIRECT_INDEX*COVID		0.0453				
OC_INDEX			0.0031			
OC_INDEX*COVID			-0.0147			
POWER_INDEX				0.0048		
POWER_INDEX*COVID				-0.0999		
AGE					0.1154*	
AGE*COVID					-0.1126	
FIRM_TENURE						-0.1209*
FIRM_TENURE*COVID						-0.0913
LN_TOTASS	0.0022	0.0055	0.0027	0.0040	0.0013	0.0067
ROA	-0.958***	-0.955***	-0.956***	-0.955***	-0.964***	-0.956***
CURRENT_RATIO	-0.0038***	-0.0036**	-0.0036**	-0.0036**	-0.0037**	-0.0030*
TAT	0.0601***	0.0588***	0.0596***	0.0599***	0.0547***	0.0595***
GROWTH	0.0355	0.0247	0.0336	0.0331	0.0325	0.0292
R-squared	0.3449	0.3576	0.3435	0.3455	0.3501	0.3630
F-statistic	18.8206	19.9022	18.7024	18.8709	19.2583	20.3704
Prob (F-statistic)	0.0000	0.0000	0.0000	0.0000	0.0000	0.0000

Note: The t-statistics are in parentheses. *, **, and *** indicate significance at the 10%, 5%, and 1% levels, respectively.

insignificant when financial decisions are taken. It might happen due to the weak CFOs power and their impact on financial decisions.

Additionally, we find that age and firm tenure have an impact on the debt ratio, but age impact is positive, and firm tenure impact is negative. This means that the higher the age variable (the younger the CFO is) the higher the debt ratio, while the higher the firm tenure variable (more years of work for the current company), the lower the debt ratio is. Our research confirms that younger people are more likely to make more risky financial decisions (Dohmen et al., 2011). The previous research of Burney et al. (2021) for US companies or for Belgian privately held SMEs (Orens and Reheul, 2013) also provides similar results. However, these investigations refer to working capital management and cash holdings decisions, respectively. Similarly, our results suggest that the long-tenured CFOs avoid risk and thus the debt ratio is lower. It is not surprising since older executives usually have longer tenure.

What is important, the COVID-19 crisis has no impact on the debt ratio and does not change the CFOs' role and risk attitude and power (interactive impact on the debt ratio). The COVID-19 crisis did not increase the role of the CFO, but made them less impactful: the independent variable that shows impact (direct index, age, and firm tenure) when interacting with the COVID-19 crisis variable made them of no statistical significance.

Out of control variables: ROA, a current ratio of financial liquidity, and TAT show statistically significant impact. Profitability has a negative impact on the debt ratio (the higher profitability the lower the debt ratio is), current ratio has a negative impact on the debt ratio (the higher financial liquidity the lower the debt ratio is), and TAT has a positive impact (the higher relation of sales revenue to total assets the higher the debt ratio is).

In regards to profitability and liquidity, our results are in line with many previous investigations that were analysed by Czerwonka and Jaworski (2019) who used meta-analysis method. Also, their research including Polish SMEs provides similar results (Czerwonka and Jaworski, 2023). The negative association between profitability and debt ratio was confirmed by other researchers (Hang et al., 2018) conducting meta-analysis.

Our results show that the age of the CFO and tenure in the company are associated with the debt ratio, but the CFO's individual risk attitude is insignificant. We suppose that older executives due to their knowledge and experience are more aware of the negative consequences of risky decisions than the younger ones. Thus, despite their individual attitude towards risk, they make less risky decisions.

Next, we analysed if there is an association between CFO's characteristics and decisions on cash holdings. The results of our analysis are shown in Table 5.9.

All models are statistically significant (F-statistics) with R-squared higher than 0.15 which means that all variables included in the model explain 15% of the variability of the dependent variable.

Table 5.9 Regression analysis results with cash ratio (CASH_ASSET) as the dependent variable

Variable	1	2	3	4
C	0.2744***	0.2227***	0.2032***	0.2387***
COVID	0.0089	0.0122	−0.0065	0.0217
INDIRECT_INDEX	−0.1117*			
INDIRECT_INDEX*COVID	0.0396			
DIRECT_INDEX		0.0305		
DIRECT_INDEX*COVID		0.0347		
OC_INDEX			0.0444	
OC_INDEX*COVID			0.0455	
POWER_INDEX				0.0401
POWER_INDEX*COVID				0.0152
LN_TOTASS	−0.0113**	−0.0129**	−0.0124**	−0.0142***
ROA	0.1305**	0.1304**	0.1162**	0.1197**
TOTLIAB_ASSET	−0.0561*	−0.0521*	−0.0577*	−0.0563*
CURRENT_RATIO	0.0001	−0.0002	−0.0002	−0.0003
TAT	0.0118*	0.0131*	0.0126*	0.0128*
GROWTH	−0.0066	−0.0025	−0.0062	−0.0029
R-squared	0.1517	0.1466	0.1489	0.1465
F-statistic	5.6613	5.4402	5.5418	5.4367
Prob (F-statistic)	0.0000	0.0000	0.0000	0.0000

Note: The t-statistics are in parentheses. *, **, and *** indicate significance at the 10%, 5%, and 1% levels, respectively.

However, we find that only the INDIRECT_INDEX of risk attitude is statistically significant, but it negatively impacts the cash ratio. This means that the higher the indirect index (more risky attitude), the lower the cash ratio is. This result is in line with the assumption that demographic characteristics such as age, gender, education, and experience affect financial decisions. It gives evidence that demographic characteristics, which are the proxies of risk attitude, are predictors of decisions on cash reserves, i.e. more risky attitude results in lower cash holdings. It supports the precautionary motives which assume that the cash reserves are a buffer against financial constraints and bankruptcy (Ferreira and Vilela, 2004).

However, the DIRECT_INDEX of risk attitude is not significant. Again, the CFO's individual risk attitude seems to be not important while decisions on cash reserves are taken.

What is important, the COVID-19 crisis has no impact on the cash ratio and does not change the CFOs' role and risk attitude and power. This result contradicts the argument of Lian, Sepehri, and Foley (2011) who state that due to uncertainty (i.e. financial crises), companies are more likely to accumulate cash in accordance with precautionary motives.

Out of control variables: Size, ROA, debt, and TAT show a statistically significant impact. Size is negatively related to the cash ratio which means that the bigger the company, the lower the cash ratio. The negative relationship between cash holdings and size supports the trade-off theory (Ferreira and Vilela, 2004). This relationship is documented by other researchers (Dittmar et al., 2003; Ferreira and Vilela, 2004; Atif et al., 2019)

Profitability has a positive impact on cash ratio which means that companies with higher profitability have higher cash ratios. This association is also documented by some researchers (Bigelli and Sánchez-Vidal, 2012; Wawryszuk-Misztal, 2021a). It means that more profitable companies accumulate cash reserves to finance profitable investments in the future (Al-Amarneh, 2015).

The debt ratio has a negative impact on the cash ratio (the higher indebtedness the lower the cash holdings). Our results are in line with the argument that companies with high levels of debt use cash to pay indebtedness (Bates et al., 2009) and confirm two theories of cash holdings: the free cash flow hypothesis and pecking theory (Mirota and Nehrebecka, 2018). The negative association between cash holdings and leverage is also documented by Ferreira and Vilela (2004) for EMU countries and research by Naumoski and Bucevska (2022) for SEE countries.

Asset turnover ratio has a positive impact on the cash ratio (the higher the relation of sales revenue to total assets, the higher the cash holdings).

The next set of models shows which components of indexes are associated with cash ratio. The results of the regression analysis are shown in Table 5.10.

Out of the elements of indexes, there are several issues included in the indirect index that have an impact on cash holdings with statistical significance. Additional education variable (ADD EDU) positively affects the cash ratio, but this means that having no additional education (i.e. risk-taking attitude) leads to a higher cash ratio. Experience as a board member variable (EXP BOARD) negatively affects the cash ratio and this means that having any experience as a board member (i.e. risk-taking attitude) leads to a lower cash ratio. The foreign experience variable (EXP ABROAD) negatively affects the cash ratio and this means that having any foreign experience (i.e. risk-taking attitude) leads to a lower cash ratio. The number of years in the position of CFO in a general variable (Exp tenure) positively affects the cash ratio, but this means that fewer years in the position (i.e. risk-taking attitude), the higher cash holdings. The number of companies that they were in the CFO position variable (EXP_NO_FIRMS) negatively affects the cash ratio. This means that working in a bigger number of companies as CFO (i.e. risk-taking attitude) leads to a lower cash ratio.

Our results confirm that some variables used as a proxy of the CFO's education and experience affect cash-holdings decisions. However, one would expect that according to precautionary motives, risk-avoiding attitude would result in a higher cash ratio. Our research partially confirms this assumption. If the CFO has experience as a board member (EXP_BOARD) or abroad

Table 5.10 Regression analysis results with cash ratio (CASH_ASSET) as dependent variable

Variable	1	2	3	4	5
C	0.2272***	0.2663***	0.2156***	0.1564**	0.2651***
COVID	0.0238	0.0276	0.0244	−0.0036	0.0298
ADD_EDU	0.0379*				
ADD_EDU*COVID	0.0185				
EXP_BOARD		−0.0287**			
EXP_BOARD*COVID		−0.0023			
EXP_ABR			−0.0397*		
EXP_ABR*COVID			0.0192		
EXP_TENURE				0.0962***	
EXP_TENURE*COVID				0.0462	
EXP_NOFIRM					−0.0814**
EXP_NOFIRM*COVID					−0.0130
LN_TOTASS	−0.0124**	−0.0133***	−0.0103**	−0.0110**	−0.0136***
ROA	0.1218**	0.1281**	0.1301**	0.1176**	0.1361***
TOTLIAB_ASSET	−0.0506	−0.0550*	−0.0563*	−0.0589*	−0.0493
CURRENT_RATIO	−0.0005	−0.0001	−0.0001	0.0001	−0.0002
TAT	0.0118*	0.0077	0.0133*	0.0129*	0.0103
GROWTH	−0.0034	−0.0051	−0.0061	−0.0098	−0.0063
R-squared	0.1592	0.1640	0.1499	0.1966	0.1637
F-statistic	5.9969	6.2113	5.5855	7.7509	6.1994
Prob (F-statistic)	0.0000	0.0000	0.0000	0.0000	0.0000

Note: The t-statistics are in parentheses. *, **, and *** indicate significance at the 10%, 5%, and 1% levels, respectively.

experience (EXP_ABROAD), or working in a bigger number of companies as CFO (EXP_NOFIRMS), he is more likely to reduce cash reserves. However, the coefficient values for the next two variables: ADD EDU and EXP TeNURE contradict the precautionary motive of holding cash. The lack of additional education or the lower number of years as CFO means that the company holds higher cash reserves.

What is important, the COVID-19 crisis variable makes statistically significant issues not significant. This means that the COVID-19 crisis made CFOs less impactful: the independent variable that shows impact when interacting with the COVID-19 crisis variable made them of no statistical significance.

Finally, we analysed if CFO's characteristics are associated with financial performance. Table 5.11 shows the results of regression analysis.

All models are statistically significant (F-statistics) with R-squared higher than 0.40 which means that all variables included in the model explain 40% of the variability of the dependent variable.

However, we find that none of the indexes of risk attitude or power is statistically significant. What is important, the COVID-19 crisis has no impact on profitability and does not change the CFOs' role and risk attitude and power but also their interactive impact on the cash ratio.

Table 5.11 Regression analysis results with ROA as dependent variable

Variable	1	2	3	4	5
C	0.1003	0.1409*	0.1157	0.1296*	0.0938
COVID	0.0103	0.0370	−0.0340	0.0234	0.0908*
INDIRECT_INDEX	0.0882				
INDIRECT_INDEX*COVID	−0.0197				
DIRECT_INDEX		−0.0288			
DIRECT_INDEX*COVID		−0.0805			
OC_INDEX			0.0288		
OC_INDEX*COVID			0.0468		
POWER_INDEX				0.0444	
POWER_INDEX*COVID				−0.0550	
AGE					0.0727*
AGE*COVID					−0.1267*
LN_TOTASS	−0.0002	0.0014	0.0003	−0.0006	0.0000
TOTLIAB_ASSET	−0.3463***	−0.3501***	−0.3455***	−0.3465***	−0.3486***
CURRENT_RATIO	−0.002*	−0.002*	−0.002*	−0.002*	−0.002*
TAT	0.050***	0.049***	0.049***	0.049***	0.047***
GROWTH	0.047***	0.042**	0.045***	0.048***	0.046***
R-squared	0.4139	0.4174	0.4126	0.4121	0.4185
F-statistic	25.2441	25.6091	25.1165	25.0550	25.7341
Prob (F-statistic)	0.0000	0.0000	0.0000	0.0000	0.0000

Note: The t-statistics are in parentheses. *, **, and *** indicate significance at the 10%, 5%, and 1% levels, respectively.

Out of the elements of indexes, we find only one element of indirect index – age – is statistically significant and shows a positive impact – which means that the higher, the age variable (the younger the CFO is) the higher profitability. But the COVID-19 crisis changes the impact of the age variable into negative which means that during COVID-19, the lower the age variable (the older CFO is), the higher profitability.

Assuming that younger CFOs are more likely to make risky decisions, our study gives evidence that a more risky attitude increases the return on assets. This association is in line with the risk-return trade-off principle. This result is in line with an investigation of SMEs in the U.K. (Shehata et al., 2017). However, the uncertainty inverts this relationship, i.e. the risk-avoidance behaviours are awarded by higher profitability.

Out of control variables debt ratio, current ratio of financial liquidity, sales to total assets, and growth show statistically significant impact on profitability. While the debt ratio and the current ratio have a negative impact on profitability, the sales to total assets and growth show a positive impact on profitability.

To sum up our regression analysis, we find little impact of CFOs' risk attitude characteristics (both direct and indirect) on financial decisions and firm performance. If any impact was found, the direction of this impact was quite opposite to our expectations. A CFO's individual risk attitude might be insignificant when financial decisions are taken. It might happen due to the weak CFO's low impact on financial decisions.

Additionally, we find that the COVID-19 crisis does not impact financial decisions and firm performance. But also we find that the COVID-19 crisis does not increase the impact of CFOs characteristics.

***

This chapter was devoted to finding the impact of the CFO on the financial decisions and firm performance. We find that financial decisions and firm performance differ with the different characteristics of the CFOs. Male forever director works for a bigger company, with lower growth, a higher debt ratio, lower cash holdings, and a lower profitability. Similarly, a young and ambitious male works for a bigger company, with low growth, lower debt ratio, high cash holdings, and higher profitability. A loyal female accountant works for a small company, with quite high growth, a lower debt ratio and cash ratio, and low profitability. And female family member works for a small company with quite high growth, with a lower debt ratio, high cash ratio, and higher profitability.

However, our regression analysis provides little evidence of the impact of CFOs' risk attitude characteristics (both direct and indirect) on financial decisions and firm performance. If any impact was found, the direction of this impact was quite opposite to our expectations. A CFO's individual risk attitude might be insignificant when financial decisions are taken. It might happen due to the low CFO's power.

Additionally, the COVID-19 crisis does not increase the impact of CFO characteristics on financial decisions and firm performance.

6 Chief financial officer – report from the field

Although our research is conducted on Polish CFOs, we believe that we provide a general picture of the CFO's role in the company. The globalization leads to the unification of financial markets and financial management. Internationalization and especially fundraising on developed capital markets require executives (and especially CFOs) to have similar skills, experience, and knowledge. Nowadays, the CFOs can gain education and experience in an international environment. More and more often, CFOs have to meet the hiring criteria set by foreign investors. At the same time, both globalization and internationalization spread the knowledge of the CFOs' duties in challenging environments. Therefore, it is expected that the result of the research including Polish CFOs might be valid in the global context. Our investigation reveals both similarities and differences between surveyed Polish CFOs and persons taking these positions in other countries.

In terms of gender, our research sample is diversified since it includes 79 men and 76 women. Our sample is quite different from those already investigated in previous research including companies from the US, China, and Sweden. Gupta et al. (2020) got the sample where female CFOs represented 8% of their sample. In Luo et al. (2020) sample there were 29% of CFO females. Nasution and Jonnergård (2017) have female CFOs share stating 17% of their sample. However, our research covers mostly private companies and this might be an explanation for the relatively high CFO women representation.

In our sample, the average age is 47 years old. This is consistent with previous findings. In Ginesti et al. (2021) sample that includes European companies, the average age is 51, with a minimum of 41 and a maximum of 63. For Chinese companies, Luo et al. (2020) find a mean and median of 44.

Education is the next demographic feature used in research on CFOs. In our sample, 99% of CFOs have at least a bachelor's degree. It is obvious that the CFO has to have a university degree which is in line with previous research for Chinese (Dong et al., 2020; Luo et al., 2020) and Indonesian companies (Frischanita and Bernawati, 2020).

Existing previous research does not tackle the CFO's educational background in such a detailed way as we did. However, the research for Greece

DOI: 10.4324/9781003473190-7

companies of Pavlatos and Kostakis (2018) find CFO's educational background at the level of 0.69 by dividing the years spent in business programs by the total years of studies. They define business-orientated studies as Business Management, Economics, Marketing, Accounting, etc., while non-business-orientated studies as Engineering, Architecture, Chemistry, Biology, etc. Calculating Pavlatos and Kostakis (2018) ratio for our sample gives us the result of 0.93 and this is a much higher ratio.

For European companies, Ginesti et al. (2021) find the CFO's educational background at a mean level of 0.3611 and a median of 0.4810, where 1 if a CFO holds an MBA or Ph.D. and 0 otherwise. Similar results were by Caglio et al. (2018) who find the CFO's educational background at a mean level of 0.47 and median of 0.5, where 1 is if the CFO has an MBA, 0 otherwise. This research proves that almost half of the sample have an MBA or Ph.D. Our sample shows a lower ratio of MBA (12%), but our sample covers both public and private companies, while previous research covers mostly public European companies. However, more than 90% of our sample of Polish CFOs have additional education. Also, other researchers show that holding a managerial position requires constant improvement of qualifications. Bernard et al. (2015) find that in their sample including the US companies, there are 49.4% of the CFOs are CPAs (Certified Public Accountants, certified accountants), 38% of the CFOs have MBA degrees, and 1% hold a CFA designation. Alrazi et al. (2018) find that 12% of their Malaysian CFO sample for postgraduate education, and 88% had a CPA certificate.

Existing previous research also tackles the issue of the number of years in the CFO position – tenure. Donatella and Tagesson (2021) find that for Swedish companies, the average CFO tenure is 6 years with a maximum of 37 years. Muttakin et al. (2019) who analysed Australian companies found the average CFO tenure of 5 years and a median of 4 years. Long tenure means a better understanding of the company – its culture, and resources. It also means better communication abilities (Bell et al., 2011; Kagzi and Guha, 2018a, Wawryszuk-Misztal, 2021a). Our sample reflects quite a long tenure – twice longer than in existing research. However, too long a tenure in one company might lead to some negative results such as groupthink syndromes, increasing risk aversion, and increasing change resistance (Bantel and Jackson, 1989; Kagzi and Guha, 2018a).

Previous professional experience is the next characteristic that describes the CFOs. In our sample of Polish CFOs, the percentage of persons with previous professional experience of a specific financial type is 54%. The CFOs' path career that includes working in audit, consulting, or financial sector is also documented by other researchers. For Nigerian companies, Ojeka et al. (2019) find that among CFOs they researched, there are 61% with experience in an audit company and 32% with experience in a consulting company. However, in the research for the US companies, Bernard et al. (2015) find that 7% of their CFOs have experience in investment banking.

International work experience is not common among Polish CFOs. Our research reveals that only 15% of the sample has working experience abroad. It contradicts with the results of Wen et al. (2020) for Chinese companies, who analysed the number of observations having at least one director with foreign experience and they find that in 2001, there were 16.62% of such observations, while in 2016, there were 47.95%. This means that international work experience become more important in recent years.

Our investigation shows that only 17 people (11% of the sample) have a stake in the company. What is more, 15 people got less than 6% stake. Also, other investigations show a relatively low shareholdings ratio. For example, Mobbs (2011) finds for the US companies that their CFO ownership mean is 0.17% with a median of 0.03%. Duong and Evans (2015) find their CFO ownership mean is 0.19% and median 0.03%. Our sample findings are lower than in previous research, but we included in our sample both public and private companies, while in most of the research, the public companies are the subject of the research.

The CFO might be a member of the board. In our sample, 34% of the respondents are members of the board of directors, and 66% are not. For Australian companies, Duong and Evans (2015) reported that almost 43% of their CFOs are members of the board of directors, while Muttakin et al. (2019) found a low level of the presence of CFO on the board with a mean of 7.2% and median of 0.0.

Referring to the role of CFOs described as Strategist, Operator, Steward, and Catalyst, our research reveals that CFOs perceive their role mostly as strategic, but their daily routine is mostly devoted to traditional activities (i.e. Operator and Steward). It is not in line with the research for other countries. For example, in 2013, Deloitte questioned CFOs across the United States, Canada, and Mexico on these four kinds of duties (Deloitte, 2013). The division of time of CFOs' interaction with their CEOs and other business units might be described as follows:

- time spent as a Strategist remains high: 31% of CFOs' time is spent working as a driver of strategy;
- time spent as an Operator rebounded since 2011: 23% of CFOs' time is spent focusing on the finance organization's efficiency and service levels/ effectiveness;
- time spent as a Catalyst declined: 24% of CFOs' time is spent working as an agent for change;
- time spent as a Steward continued to fall: 22% of CFOs' time is spent overseeing accounting, control, risk management, and asset preservation.

The four faces of the CFO reflect the theoretical and desired role of the CFO, but the practice is quite different. The practical aspect of the CFO role is presented in existing research.

There are many surveys reflecting the role of the financial director (FD/CFO): the survey for Europe, the Middle East, India, and Africa (Ernst and Young, 2013), Canada, the US, Mexico, and Brazil (Ernst and Young, 2012), Canada (Beyond the Numbers, 2011), Singapore (Kai, 1996), and China (Deloitte, 2012).

One of the surveys was carried out by Ernst and Young in 2010 and in 2011 among a group of more than 530 CFOs from EMEIA – Europe, the Middle East, India, and Africa (Ernst and Young, 2012). While the emphasis certainly varies by organization – and depends in part on factors such as the organization's competitive position and the prevailing economic environment – the report highlighted six principal activities that fairly represent the contribution of today's top finance executives. They are the following: 1) ensuring business decisions are grounded in solid financial criteria, 2) providing insight and analysis to support the CEO and other senior managers, 3) leading key initiatives in finance that support overall strategic goals, 4) funding, enabling, and executing the strategy set by the CEO, 5) developing and defining the overall strategy for the organization, and 6) representing the organization's progress on strategic goals to external stakeholders.

In this survey across EMEIA, almost 60% of 669 CFO respondents judged themselves to play a key role in "providing insight and analysis to support the CEO and other senior managers in strategic planning." And 49% of them said they play a key role in "leading key initiatives that support overall strategy," and in "ensuring business decisions are grounded in sound financial criteria." About 56% of the EMEIA respondents said that other managers across the business routinely turn to finance for advice on strategy. More than 60% say the visibility and respect accorded finance has improved in the last three years. This perspective is largely corroborated by the participants in the Americas, who also suggest that CFOs play an important role in providing a financial perspective on operational challenges, and can prompt internal changes or help drive initiatives that improve the business.

Another survey was conducted in 2011 of 263 senior financial executives across Canada (Beyond the numbers, 2011). The leading responsibilities of the CFO as seen by financial executives were three-fold: financial reporting and accounting (98%); supporting executive team decision-making (97%); and budgeting and forecasting (also 97%). Tax compliance/planning (86%) and risk management (85%) were duties shouldered by slightly fewer CFOs, according to survey participants, followed by corporate governance (71%). Not surprisingly, evaluating M&As (65%); corporate finance and public markets (63%), board advisor (59%), and the integration of M&As (51%), were not universal as CFO's responsibilities in these areas would depend on the type and situation of the organization at a particular time. In addition, 41% of CFOs were also responsible for operations. The majority (78%) of CFOs believe they are currently fulfilling this "strategic CFO" role to some degree. When asked to define the role the CFO has in the strategic planning process, nearly half of all finance executives surveyed said the CFO at their organization is involved in setting strategic direction along with other members of the senior management team. About one-third said the CFO acts as a strategic advisor to the management team, including providing business advice and input beyond financial implications.

Deloitte's surveys of Chief Financial Officers refer to major Irish-based companies. The survey was conducted in March 2013, and CFOs of listed companies, large private companies, and Irish subsidiaries of overseas multinational companies participated (Deloitte, 2013). Managing company performance clearly presents the greatest challenge for CFOs. 40% of respondents identified company performance as the top challenge with the multiplicity of stakeholder relationships ranked as the second most challenging aspect of the CFO's role (20%). Dealing with uncertainty follows closely behind the top two challenges as 16% of CFOs consider economic or strategic ambiguity to be the third most challenging aspect of their role. 88% of CFOs recognize the need to place greater emphasis on managing change to drive business transformation and evaluate and execute strategies. This reflects the expanding role of the CFO and the growing involvement in strategy and change initiatives. Similarly, 82% of respondents are placing greater emphasis on developing relationships with senior executives and alignment on strategic decision-making and financial objectives. Risk is also a priority for CFOs reflecting the continuously uncertain market conditions. 65% of respondents recognize the need to place greater emphasis on their role as a gatekeeper of risk and the requirement to provide a financial perspective to risk management. Transaction processing (27%), followed by consolidate, close, and report (23%), and performance and decisions (19%) are considered to be the top three most time-consuming activities performed by the finance function. This indicates that the more traditional aspects of the CFO's role continue to constitute the greatest portion of a CFO's time. As the finance function evolves and interacts with organizational functions, CFOs are increasingly involved in influencing non-financial as well as financial measures. This is reflected by survey respondents as 94% of CFOs disagree with having finance focused solely on financial reporting. At the same time, 59% of respondents believe that the finance function spends too much time on financial and management reporting rather than understanding what is driving the business. 64% of CFOs believe that business managers have a good set of key performance indicators (financial and non-financial to aid decision-making). In addition, 94% of those surveyed believe that the finance function has a good understanding of the organization's future expected performance. The expanding role of the CFO to incorporate a greater emphasis on strategy and overall company performance represents a key theme, reflecting the evolving role of the CFO and the finance function. CFOs are also confident in their ability to manage and be involved in the strategic direction of the organization, underpinned by the 94% of respondents who believe that the finance function has a good understanding of the organization's future expected performance. The need to juggle various initiatives including organizational change and transformation will continue to grow in importance for CFOs, diminishing the time spent on traditional finance activities such as transaction processing, consolidation, closing, and reporting activities.

Another survey was carried out in Singapore in the 1990s. The data was collected after surveying 42 organizations (Kai, 1996). Their main fields of duties refer to taxation (60%), financial management and financial performance (58%), treasury operations (57%), management information systems (preparing and interpreting management accounts (50%), corporate strategy and setting financial strategic objectives (40%), and M&A and divestment (32%).

The research carried out by Wawryszuk-Misztal and Wrońska-Bukalska (2014) for Polish companies assumed the analysis of the job advertisement content posted on the web portal with job offers. The advertisements were placed directly by enterprises seeking candidates for the post of chief financial officer (CFO) as well as by headhunting agencies which were commissioned by their clients to carry out recruitment. In particular, the scope of responsibilities assigned to the post of the CFO was the subject of the detailed analysis. The tasks of the CFO presented in the analysed advertisements were grouped. Special attention was put to the tasks connected with the CFO's participation in the creation and execution of the company's strategy. In 25% of the analysed advertisements' cases, the CFO was expected to cooperate and realize the strategy in the area of finances, which, in some advertisements, was referred to as either strategy or financial policy. It is also expected that the CFO will provide substantial support for the decisions taken by the Board of Directors (27% of cases), which primarily involves preparing reports and analysis necessary to make decisions by the Board, and which was pointed out by as many as 69% of employers. The CFO's tasks may also involve managing operating profitability, and, in particular, seeking and indicating solutions which are to foster the increase in profitability (31% of the advertisements) through, among others, carrying out the analysis of margins gained by particular products, as well as determining the price of sales. Another important area of the CFO's performance is tax management viewed not only as overseeing the accuracy of clearings done with tax offices, but, first of all, as undertaking those activities which foster tax optimization (33% of cases). In 92% of advertisements specifying the tasks of the CFO, participation or oversight of the planning process and budgeting were recognized as his/her assignments, but then more often these tasks were connected with budgeting rather and variance analysis than creating financial planning. Among activities defined as financial planning and budgeting, one may point to one area which may be referred to as cost management. In 38% of cases of the analysed advertisements, the CFO is expected to create the cost budget, carry out the cost variance analysis against adopted forecasts, and consequently, come up with solutions that would optimize the level of costs in the company. Traditionally, the role of the CFO is to assess the profitability of investment projects, which is indicated in 27% of cases, and raise funds (33% of cases), as well as overviewing its use especially when such resources were received from the EU. Raising funds quite often means responsibility for carrying out an Initial Public Offer on the WSE (Warsaw Stock Exchange), which was also pointed out by the advertisers. The assignments of the CFO also lie in managing liquidity which was expected in 58% of the reviewed advertisements. Generally, as it was also presumed, another significant area of the CEO activities is overseeing accountancy and, specifically, overseeing the process of creating financial reporting as well as other documentation in compliance with the governing laws (86% of cases). A wide range of duties arising from performing a function of the CFO makes him/her obligated to maintain relations with external institutions (tax offices, banks, and GUS – the Main Statistical Office), or with investors, and the oversight of making up documentation to meet the requirements as was shown in 65% of the analysed advertisements. Risk management is yet another area related to finances, though in only 15% of the analysed advertisements such activities are viewed to be assigned to the CFO's responsibilities. Performing managerial functions undoubtedly requires that the CFOs have competencies to manage the subordinate staff of the financial, accounting controlling departments, and others (50% of the analysed advertisements).

According to all of this research, CEOs expect CFOs more involvement in strategy setting, strategy execution, and strategy development support. Less important were investment management, capital, performance, and liquidity management. The least important was reporting. Undoubtedly, it seems that the role of the FD/CFO should no longer be what it was before. In each of the surveyed countries, from Europe, the Middle East, Africa, India, China, Brazil, Mexico, and the US to Canada, the role is no longer a simple, functional position but has evolved into a strategic one. The CFO is not only an accountant, but also a strategy creator.

***

This chapter provides a discussion of our findings with previous research on CFOs from different countries. We think that our research contributes to the rather modest amount of research on the role of CFOs. We provide evidence on CFOs in Poland, the biggest economy in Central and Eastern Europe, with the greatest progress in the transition process to become a developed financial market and mature economy.

We find several differences but also similarities of Polish CFOs with CFOs from other countries. However, we believe that despite the diverse institutional backgrounds, the role of CFOs will grow. Our work shows that the investigation on behavioural aspects of financial decisions should be continued. Because our research includes only Polish CFOs, we recommend conducting similar research in other countries and including other variables such as the features of CEOs.

Summary

The aim of our research was to find the relationship between the CFOs' characteristics and financial decisions (cash holdings and capital structure), and then analyse if the CFOs' individual characteristics are associated with the firm's financial performance. Our research is based on the presumption that the role of the financial director has changed recently. Several studies prove that the CFO's demographic characteristics play a key role in determining financial decisions and firm performance.

The main tool to collect the data on demographic characteristics was a survey. This allows us to provide new insight into the people and processes behind corporate decisions. Our survey quantifies the behavioural traits of senior executives and also harvests information related to career paths, education, and demographics. We also ask questions related to standard corporate finance decisions such as leverage policy, debt maturity, and acquisition activity. This allows us to relate attitudes and managerial attributes to corporate actions.

We sent the survey questionnaire to a great number of CFOs. However, there is a big reluctance among business practitioners to provide answers and be involved in the research. As a result, we got 155 answers from the CFOs both in private and public companies. Our sample is quite diversified in terms of age, gender, education, and professional background.

What is important, all surveyed CFOs believe they have a big impact on strategic decisions such as long-term plans and investment decisions but the biggest on raising capital, cash management, and financial statement preparation. At the same time, they admit that most of their daily activities are connected with those characteristics of Steward. They also present similar attitudes towards risk in financial decision-making. This does not change if we take into account age and gender.

This led us to further investigate of differences between CFOs. Thus, we decided to create four clusters depending on age, gender, education, and previous professional experience. We were able to find male forever directors, female loyal accountants, young and ambitious male directors, and female family members. However, their perception of the impact on financial

DOI: 10.4324/9781003473190-8

decisions does not differ significantly. Female family members spend more time on strategic activities. The riskiest attitude is presented by forever directors, then young and ambitious directors; also a loyal accountant is risky but female family members show a low-risk attitude. We find that each type of CFO works for a different type of company: a male forever director works for a bigger company, with lower growth, a higher debt ratio, lower cash holdings, and lower profitability. Similarly, a young and ambitious male works for a bigger company, with low growth, lower debt ratio, high cash holdings, and higher profitability. While a loyal female accountant works for a small company, with quite high growth, a lower debt ratio and cash ratio, and low profitability. And female family member works for a small company with quite high growth, with a lower debt ratio, high cash ratio, and higher profitability. Our results confirm the assumption that CFO's demographic characteristics might be important for financial decisions and financial performance.

Then, we develop three indexes of the CFO's risk attitude (one direct and two indirect) and one index of the CFO's power. The direct index is based on the CFOs' attitude towards financial decisions (whether they choose more or less risky financial decisions). One of the indirect indexes is based on demographic characteristics (age, gender, education, professional experience), and another on overconfidence. Additionally, the power index reflects the CFO's tenure, position on the board of directors, and stake in the company. However, we find that their demographic characteristics, attitude towards risk, or behavioural biases are not important for their perception of the impact on financial decisions. The most important factor affecting their perception of high impact on strategic decisions is their power. But none of the indexes are important in shaping their time activities allotment. It seems that no matter what is their attitude towards risk and what is their power, their daily activities are the same.

However, our regression analysis provides little evidence of the impact of CFOs' risk attitude characteristics (both direct and indirect) on financial decisions and firm performance. If any impact was found, the direction of this impact was quite opposite to our expectations. A CFO's individual risk attitude might be insignificant when financial decisions are taken. These findings are consistent with the notion that the CFO is more a Steward and Operator than a Strategist or Catalyst. This means that there is more stewardship role for the CFOs. This is in line with previous findings on CFOs as "bean counters" and their subordinate position to the CEO (Hiebl, 2013b; Hiebl, 2015).

References

Aboody, D., & Kasznik, R. (2000). CEO stock option awards and the timing of corporate voluntary disclosures. *Journal of Accounting and Economics, 29*(1), 73–100. https://doi.org/73-100./10.1016/S0165-4101(00)00014-8

Adams, R. B., & Ferreira, D. (2007). A theory of friendly boards. *Journal of Finance, 62*(1), 217–250. https://doi.org/10.1111/j.1540-6261.2007.01206.x

Adams, R. B., & Ferreira, D. (2009). Women in the boardroom and their impact on governance and performance. *Journal of Financial Economics, 94*(2), 291–309. https://doi.org/10.1016/j.jfineco.2008.10.007

Adhikari, B. K. (2018). Female executives and corporate cash holdings. *Applied Economics Letters, 25*(13), 958–963. https://doi.org/10.1080/13504851.2017.1388904

Al-Amarneh, A. (2015). Corporate cash holdings and financial crisis: Evidence from Jordan. *International Business Research, 8*(5), 212–220. https://doi.org/10.5539/ibr.v8n5p212

Aldubhani, M. A. Q., Wang, J., Gong, T., & Maudhah, R. A. (2022). Impact of working capital management on profitability: Evidence from listed companies in Qatar. *Journal of Money and Business, 2*(1), 70–81. https://doi.org/10.1108/jmb-08-2021-0032

Almeida, N. S., & Lemes, S. (2020). Determinants of accounting choice: Do CFOs' characteristics matter? *Management Research Review, 43*(2), 185–203. https://doi.org/10.1108/MRR-02-2019-0076

Alrazi, B., Husin, N. M., & Ali, I. M. (2018). Does CFO expertise matter? A case of corporate water reporting among Malaysian public listed companies. *Global Business & Management Research: An International Journal, 10*(3), 239–248.

Altman, D. (2002, April 11). The taming of the finance officers. *New York Times*, 10–11.

Anderson, R. C., Reeb, D. M., Upadhyay, A., & Zhao, W. (2011). The economics of director heterogeneity. *Financial Management, 40*(1), 5–38. https://doi.org/10.1111/j.1755-053X.2010.01133.x

Ararat, M., Aksu, M., & Tansel Cetin, A. (2015). How board diversity affects firm performance in emerging markets: Evidence on channels in controlled firms. *Corporate Governance: An International Review, 23*(2), 83–103. https://doi.org/10.1111/corg.12103

Arnaldi, A., Novak, B., Roscigno, R., & Zhang, W. (2021). Working capital management and profitability: Empirical evidence international. *Journal of Business Management and Economic Research (IJBMER), 12*(2), 1911–1917.

Atif, M., Liu, B., & Huang, A. (2019). Does board gender diversity affect corporate cash holdings? *Journal of Business Finance and Accounting, 46*(7–8), 1003–1029. https://doi.org/10.1111/jbfa.12397

Baker, T. A., Lopez, T. J., Reitenga, A. L., & Ruch, G. W. (2019). The influence of CEO and CFO power on accruals and real earnings management. *Review of Quantitative Finance and Accounting, 52*(1), 325–345.

Baker, M., & Wurgler, J. (2002). Market timing and capital structure. *Journal of Finance, 57*(1), 1–32. https://doi.org/10.1111/1540-6261.00414

Bantel, K. A., & Jackson, S. E. (1989). Top management and innovations in banking: Does the composition of the top team make a difference? *Strategic Management Journal, 10*(S1), 107–124.

Barsky, R. B., Juster, F. T., Kimball, M. S., & Shapiro, M. D. (1997). Preference parameters and behavioral heterogeneity: An experimental approach in the health and retirement study. *Quarterly Journal of Economics, 112*(2), 537–579. https://doi.org/10.1162/003355397555280

Bates, T. W., Kahle, K. M., & Stulz, R. M. (2009). Why do U.S. firms hold so much more cash than they used to? *Journal of Finance, 64*(5), 1985–2021. https://doi.org/10.1111/j.1540-6261.2009.01492.x

Beaver, W. H., Correia, M., & McNichols, M. F. (2011). Financial statement analysis and the prediction of financial distress. *Foundations and Trends(R) in Accounting, 5*(2), 99–173.

Bedard, J. C., Hoitash, R., & Hoitash, U. (2014). Chief financial officers as inside directors. *Contemporary Accounting Research, 31*(3), 787–817. https://doi.org/10.1111/1911-3846.12045

Bell, S. T., Villado, A. J., Lukasik, M. A., Belau, L., & Briggs, A. L. (2011). Getting specific about demographic diversity variable and team performance relationships: A meta-analysis. *Journal of Management, 37*(3), 709–743.

Bernard, D., Ge, W., Matsumoto, D., & Toynbee, S. (2015). *Are there costs to hiring an accounting expert CFO*. (Working paper). Washington, US: University of Washington.

Berry, S. G., Betterton, C. E., & Karagiannidis, I. (2014). Understanding weighted average cost of capital: A pedagogical application. *Journal of Financial Education, 40*(1/2), 115–136.

Beyond the Numbers: The Evolving Leadership Role of the CFO (2011). Canadian Financial Executives Research Foundation, Toronto. https://www.feicanada.org/enews/file/CFERF%20studies/2010-2011/CFERF%20role%20of%20the%20cfo%20final.pdf(15.11.2014).

Bigelli, M., & Sánchez-Vidal, J. (2012). Cash holdings in private firms. *Journal of Banking and Finance, 36*(1), 26–35. https://doi.org/10.1016/j.jbankfin.2011.06.004

Bolek, M., Pluskota, A., & Wolski, R. (2021). Liquidity – Profitability trade-off on the example of companies listed on main and alternative new connect markets on Warsaw Stock Exchange. *Finanse i Prawo Finansowe, 4*(28), 7–24. https://doi.org/10.18778/2391-6478.s.2021.01

Brammer, S., Millington, A., & Pavelin, S. (2007). Gender and ethnic diversity among UK corporate boards. *Corporate Governance: An International Review, 15*(2), 393–403. https://doi.org/10.1111/j.1467-8683.2007.00569.x

Brealey, R. A., Myers, S. C., Allen, F., & Mohanty, P. (2012). *Principles of corporate finance*. New York: McGraw-Hill/Irwin.

Brown, R., & Sarma, N. (2007). CEO overconfidence, CEO dominance and corporate acquisitions. *Journal of Economics and Business, 59*(5), 358–379. https://doi.org/10.1016/j.jeconbus.2007.04.002

Bugg, J. M., Zook, N. A., DeLosh, E. L., Davalos, D. B., & Davis, H. P. (2006). Age differences in fluid intelligence: Contributions of general slowing and frontal decline. *Brain and Cognition, 62*(1), 9–16. https://doi.org/10.1016/j.bandc.2006.02.006

Bukalska, E. (2020). Are companies managed by overconfident CEO financially constraint? Investment–cash flow sensitivity approach. *Equilibrium. Quarterly Journal of Economics and Economic Policy, 15*(1), 107–131. https://doi.org/10.24136/eq.2020.006

Burney, R. B., James, H. L., & Wang, H. (2021). Working capital management and CEO age. *Journal of Behavioral and Experimental Finance, 30*, 100496. https://doi.org/10.1016/j.jbef.2021.100496

Byrnes, J. P., Miller, D. C., & Schafer, W. D. (1999). Gender differences in risk taking: A meta-analysis. *Psychological Bulletin, 125*(3), 367–383. https://doi.org/10.1037/0033-2909.125.3.367

Caglio, A., Dossi, A., & Van der Stede, W. A. (2018). CFO role and CFO compensation: An empirical analysis of their implications. *Journal of Accounting and Public Policy, 37*(4), 265–281, https://doi.org/10.1016/j.jaccpubpol.2018.07.002

Cai, Y., & Li, M. (2022). CEO-CFO tenure consistency and cash holdings. *Emerging Markets Finance and Trade, 58*(12), 3554–3566. https://doi.org/10.1080/1540496X.2022.2058929

Cambrea, D. R., Tenuta, P., & Vastola, V. (2019). Female directors and corporate cash holdings: Monitoring vs executive roles. *Management Decision, 58*(2), 295–312. https://doi.org/10.1108/MD-11-2018-1289

Camelo, C., Fernández-Alles, M., & Hernández, A. B. (2010). Strategic consensus, top management teams, and innovation performance. *International Journal of Manpower, 31*(6), 678–695. https://doi.org/10.1108/01437721011073373

Canace, T. G. (2014). CFO: From analyst to catalyst. *Strategic Finance, 95*(8), 27–33.

Carpenter, M. A., Geletkanycz, M. A., & Sanders, W. G. (2004). Upper echelons revisited: Antecedents, elements, and consequences of top management team composition. *Journal of Management, 30*(6), 749–778. https://doi.org/10.1016/j.jm.2004.06.001

Carson, C. (2012). The Role of the CFO in the NZ Public Sector: Steward, Operator, Strategist, Catalyst and Trusted Advocate. http://www.conferenz.co.nz/whitepapers/the-role-of-the-cfo-in-the-nzpublic-sector-steward-operator-strategist-catalyst-and-tru(22.06.2016)

Caselli, S., & Di Giuli, A. (2010). Does the CFO matter in family firms? Evidence from Italy. *European Journal of Finance, 16*(5), 381–411. https://doi.org/10.1080/13518470903211657

Chava, S., & Purnanandam, A. (2010). CEOs versus CFOs: Incentives and corporate policies. *Journal of Financial Economics, 97*(2), 263–278. https://doi.org/10.1016/j.jfineco.2010.03.018

Copeland, T. E., Weston, J. F., & Shastri, K. (2005). *Financial theory and corporate policy*. Boston: Pearson Addison Wesley.

Croson, R., & Gneezy, U. (2009). Gender differences in preferences. *Journal of Economic Literature, 47*(2), 448–474. https://doi.org/10.1257/jel.47.2.448

Custódio, C., Ferreira, M. A., & Matos, P. (2013). Generalists versus specialists: Lifetime work experience and chief executive officer pay. *Journal of Financial Economics, 108*(2), 471–492.

Czerwonka, L., & Jaworski, J. (2019). Meta-study on relationship between macroeconomic and institutional environment and internal determinants of enterprises' capital structure. *Economic Research-Ekonomska Istrazivanja, 32*(1), 2614–2637. https://doi.org/10.1080/1331677X.2019.1650653

Czerwonka, L., & Jaworski, J., (2023). Which capital structure theory explains financial behavior of small and medium-sized enterprises? Evidence from Poland. *Gospodarka Narodowa. The Polish Journal of Economics, 313*(1), 82–92. https://doi.org/10.33119/GN/159035

Darmadi, S. (2013). Board members' education and firm performance: Evidence from a developing economy. *International Journal of Commerce and* Management, 23(2), 113–135. https://doi.org/10.1108/10569211311324911

Datta, S., Doan, T., Guha, A., Iskandar-Datta, M., & Kwon, M. J. (2023). CFO credentials, stock market signaling, and firm performance. *International Journal of Managerial Finance, 19*(3), 539–571. https://doi.org/10.1108/IJMF-11-2021-0571

Datta, S., & Iskandar-Datta, M. (2014). Upper-echelon executive human capital and compensation: Generalist vs specialist skills. *Strategic Management Journal, 35*(12), 1853–1866. https://doi.org/10.1002/smj.2267

Dauth, T., Pronobis, P., & Schmid, S. (2017). Exploring the link between internationalization of top management and accounting quality: The CFO's international experience matters. *International Business Review, 26*(1), 71–88. https://doi.org/10.1016/j.ibusrev.2016.05.007

Davis, J. H., Schoorman, F. D., & Donaldson, L. (1997). Toward a stewardship theory of management. *The Academy of Management Review, 22*(1), 20–47. https://doi.org/10.2307/259223

De Meulenaere, K., Boone, C., & Buyl, T. (2016). Unraveling the impact of workforce age diversity on labor productivity: The moderating role of firm size and job security. *Journal of Organizational Behavior, 37*(2), 193–212. https://doi.org/10.1002/job.2036

Deari, F., Kukeli, A., Barbuta-Misu, N., & Virlanuta, F. O. (2022). Does working capital management affect firm profitability? Evidence from European Union countries. *Journal of Economic and Administrative Sciences,* Ahead of print. https://doi.org/10.1108/jeas-11-2021-0222

Deloitte. (2007). *The Finance Talent Challenge: How leading CFOs are taking charge* https://fpacert.afponline.org/docs/librariesprovider6/default-document-library/pdf/the-finance-talent-challenge.pdf?sfvrsn=3521466b_2(05.08.2014).

Deloitte. (2012). *China CFO Survey.* http://www2.deloitte.com(05.08.2015).

Deloitte. (2013). *CFO signals. What North America's top finance executives are thinking – and doing.* 3rd Quarter. http://deloitte.wsj.com/cfo/files(15.11.2014)

Deloof, M. (2003). Does working capital management affect profitability of Belgian firms? *Journal of Business Finance & Accounting, 30*(3–4), 573–587. https://doi.org/10.1111/1468-5957.00008.

Dichev, I. D., Graham, J. R., Harvey, C. R., & Rajgopal, S. (2013). Earnings quality: Evidence from the field. *Journal of Accounting and Economics, 56*(2–3), Supplement 1, 1–33. https://doi.org/10.1016/j.jacceco.2013.05.004

Dittmar, A., & Duchin, R. (2016). Looking in the rearview mirror: The effect of managers' professional experience on corporate financial policy. *Review of Financial Studies, 29*(3), 565–602. https://doi.org/10.1093/rfs/hhv051

Dittmar, A., Mahrt-Smith, J., & Servaes, H. (2003). International corporate governance and corporate cash holdings. *The Journal of Financial and Quantitative Analysis, 38*(1), 111–133. https://doi.org/10.2307/4126766

Doan, T., & Iskandar-Datta, M. (2020). Are female top executives more risk-averse or more ethical? Evidence from corporate cash holdings policy. *Journal of Empirical Finance*, *55*, 161–176. https://doi.org/10.1016/j.jempfin.2019.11.005

Dohmen, T., Falk, A., Golsteyn, B. H. H., Huffman, D., & Sunde, U. (2017). Risk attitudes across the life course. *Economic Journal*, *127*(605), F95–F116. https://doi.org/10.1111/ecoj.12322

Dohmen, T., Falk, A., Huffman, D., Sunde, U., Schupp, J., & Wagner, G. G. (2011). Individual risk attitudes: Measurement, determinants, and behavioral consequences. *Journal of the European Economic Association*, *9*(3), 522–550. https://doi.org/10.1111/j.1542-4774.2011.01015.x

Donatella, P., & Tagesson, T. (2021). CFO characteristics and opportunistic accounting choice in public sector organizations. *Journal of Management and Governance*, *25*(2), 509–534.

Dong, L., Wu, B., & Wang, P. (2020). Study on the relation between gender characteristics of CFO and earnings management. *IOP Conf. Series: Materials Science and Engineering Conference Series*, *768*, 072005. https://doi.org/10.1088/1757-899X/768/7/072005

Doron, M., Baker, C. R., & Zucker, K. D. (2019). Bookkeeper-controller-CFO: The rise of the chief financial and chief accounting officer. *Accounting Historians Journal*, *46*(2), 1–8. https://doi.org/10.2308/aahj-52538

Doukas, J. A., & Petmezas, D. (2007). Acquisitions, overconfident managers and self-attribution bias. *European Financial Management*, *13*(3), 531–577. https://doi.org/10.1111/j.1468-036X.2007.00371.x

Drake, P. P., & Fabozzi, F. J. (2009). *Foundations and applications of the time value of money*. Hoboken, NJ: John Wiley & Sons.

Drees, J. M., & Heugens, P. P. M. A. R. (2013). Synthesizing and extending resource dependence theory: A meta-analysis. *Journal of Management*, *39*(6), 1666–1698. https://doi.org/10.1177/0149206312471391

Dudley, E., & Zhang, N. (2016). Trust and corporate cash holdings. *Journal of Corporate Finance*, *41*, 363–387. https://doi.org/10.1016/j.jcorpfin.2016.10.010

Duong, L., & Evans, J. (2015). CFO compensation: Evidence from Australia. *Pacific-Basin Finance Journal*, *35*, 425–443. https://doi.org/10.1016/j.pacfin.2015.03.006

Duong, L., Evans, J., & Truong, T. P. (2020). Getting CFO on board – Its impact on firm performance and earnings quality. *Accounting Research Journal*, *33*(2), 435–454. https://doi.org/10.1108/ARJ-10-2018-0185

Efendi, J., Srivastava, A., & Swanson, E. P. (2007). Why do corporate managers misstate financial statements? The role of option compensation and other factors. *Journal of Financial Economics*, *85*(3), 667–708. https://doi.org/10.1016/j.jfineco.2006.05.009.

Eisenhardt, K. M. (1989). Agency theory: An assessment and review. *The Academy of Management Review*, *14*(1), 57–74. https://doi.org/10.2307/258191

Eljelly, A. M. A. (2004). Liquidity - profitability tradeoff: An empirical investigation in an emerging market. *International Journal of Commerce and Management*, *14*(2), 48–61. https://doi.org/10.1108/10569210480000179

Ernst and Young (2012). *Views. Vision. Insights. The evolving role of today's CFO. An Americas supplement to The DNA of the CFO*. http://www.ey.com/Publication/ (05.08.2015).

Ernst and Young (2013). *The DNA of the CFO*. http://www.ey.com/Publication(12.08.2015).

Eulerich, M., Velte, P., & Van Uum, C. (2014). The impact of management board diversity on corporate performance – an empirical analysis for the German two-tier system. *Problems and Perspectives in Management, 12*(1), 25–39.

Faccio, M., Marchica, M. T., & Mura, R. (2016). CEO gender, corporate risk-taking, and the efficiency of capital allocation. *Journal of Corporate Finance, 39*, 193–209. https://doi.org/10.1016/j.jcorpfin.2016.02.008

Falk, A., Becker, A., Dohmen, T., Enke, B., Huffman, D., & Sunde, U. (2018). Global evidence on economic preferences. *Quarterly Journal of Economics 133*(4), 1645–1692. https://doi.org/10.1093/qje/qjy013

Fama, E. F., & French, K. R. (2004). The capital asset pricing model: Theory and evidence. *Journal of Economic Perspectives, 18*(3), 25–46. https://doi.org/10.1257/0895330042162430

Fama, E. F., & Jensen, M. C. (1983). Separation of ownership and control. *Journal of Law and Economics 26*(2), 301–326, https://doi.org/10.1086/467037

Farag, H., & Mallin, C. (2016). The impact of the dual board structure and board diversity: Evidence from Chinese initial public offerings (IPOs). *Journal of Business Ethics, 139*, 333–349. https://doi.org/10.1007/s10551-015-2649-6

Fee, C. E., & Hadlock, C. (2004). Management turnover across the corporate hierarchy. *Journal of Accounting and Economics* 37(1), 3–38, https://doi.org/10.1016/j.jacceco.2003.11.003

Feng, M., Ge, W., Luo, S., & Shevlin, T. (2011). Why do CFOs become involved in material accounting manipulations. *Journal of Accounting and Economics. 51*(1–2), 21–36, https://doi.org/10.1016/j.jacceco.2010.09.005

Ferreira, M. A., & Vilela, A. S. (2004). Why do firms hold cash? Evidence from EMU countries. *European Financial Management, 10*(2), 295–319. https://doi.org/10.1111/j.1354-7798.2004.00251.x

Ferris, S. P., & Sainani, S. (2021). Do CFOs matter? Evidence from the M&A process. *Journal of Corporate Finance, 67*(January), 101856. https://doi.org/10.1016/j.jcorpfin.2020.101856

Fink, R. (2002, August 1). The fear of all sums. *CFO Magazine*. http://ww2.cfo.com/risk-compliance/2002/08/the-fear-of-all-sums/.

Finkelstein, S. (1992). Power in top management teams: Dimensions, measurement, and validation. *The Academy of Management Journal, 35*(3), 505–538. https://doi.org/10.2307/256485.

Florackis, C., & Sainani, S. (2018). How do chief financial officers influence corporate cash policies? *Journal of Corporate Finance, 52*, 168–191. https://doi.org/10.1016/j.jcorpfin.2018.08.001

Francis, J., Huang, A. H., Rajgopal, S., & Zang, A. Y. (2008), CEO reputation and earnings quality. *Contemporary Accounting Research, 25*(1), 109–147. https://doi.org/10.1506/car.25.1.4

Frank, M. Z., & Goyal, V. K. (2007). Corporate leverage: How much do managers really matter? *SSRN Electronic Journal*. https://doi.org/10.2139/ssrn.971082

Friedman, H. L. (2014). Implications of power: When the CEO can pressure the CFO to bias reports, *Journal of Accounting and Economics, 58*(1), 117–141. https://doi.org/10.1016/j.jacceco.2014.06.004

Frischanita, Y., & Bernawati, Y. (2020). The effect of CFO demographics on fraudulent financial reporting. *Jurnal Akuntansi, 24*(1), 21–36. https://doi.org/10.24912/ja.v24i1.639

110   References

García-Teruel, P. J., & Martínez-Solano, P. (2007). Effects of working capital management on SME profitability. *International Journal of Managerial Finance, 3*(2), 164–177. https://doi.org/10.1108/17439130710738718

Geiger, M. A., & North, D. S. (2006). Does hiring a new CFO change things? An investigation of changes in discretionary accruals. *The Accounting Review, 81*(4), 781–809. https://doi.org/10.1521/accr.2006.81.4.781

Ghosh, A., Cai, F., & Li, W. (2000). The determinants of capital structure. *American Business Review, 18*(2), 129–132.

Ginesti, G., Spanò, R., Ferri, L., & Caldarelli, A. (2021). The chief financial officer (CFO) profile and R&D investment intensity: Evidence from listed European companies. *Management Decision, 59*(13), 99–114. https://doi.org/10.1108/MD-05-2020-0650

Girigori, E. C. Z. L. (2013). *The Relationship Between CFO Expertise and Firm Performance* [Master's Thesis, Tilburg University]. https://arno.uvt.nl/show.cgi?fid=132419

Glinkowska, B., & Kaczmarek, B. (2015). Classical and modern concepts of corporate governance (Stewardship theory and agency theory). *Management, 19*(2), 84–92. https://doi.org/10.1515/manment-2015-0015

Gordini, N. (2016). Does the family status of the CFO matter to enhance family firm performance? Evidence from a sample of small and medium-sized Italian family firms. *International Journal of Entrepreneurship and Small Business, 28*(1), 36–57. https://doi.org/10.1504/IJESB.2016.075681

Graham, J., & Harvey, C. (2001). The theory and practice of corporate finance: Evidence from the field. *Journal of Financial Economics, 60*(2–3), 187–243. https://doi.org/10.1016/S0304-405X(01)00044-7

Graham, J. R., Harvey, C. R., & Puri, M. (2013). Managerial attitudes and corporate actions. *Journal of Financial Economics, 109*(1), 103–121. https://doi.org/10.1016/j.jfineco.2013.01.010

Graham, J. R., Harvey, C. R., & Puri, M. (2015). Capital allocation and delegation of decision-making authority within firms. *Journal of Financial Economics, 115*(3), 449–470. https://doi.org/10.1016/j.jfineco.2014.10.011

Graham, J. R., Harvey, C. R., & Rajgopal, S. (2005). The economic implications of corporate financial reporting. *Journal of Accounting and Economics, 40*(1–3), 3–73. https://doi.org/10.1016/j.jacceco.2005.01.002

Gray, S., & Nowland, J. (2017). The diversity of expertise on corporate boards in Australia. *Accounting & Finance, 57*(2), 429–463. https://doi.org/10.1111/acfi.12146

Gupta, M., & Aggarwal, N. (2018). Signaling effect of shifts in dividend policy: Evidence from Indian capital markets. *Business Perspectives and Research, 6*(2), 142–153. https://doi.org/10.1177/2278533718764505

Gupta, V. K., Mortal, S., Chakrabarty, B., Guo, X., & Turban, D. B. (2020). CFO gender and financial statement irregularities. *Academy of Management Journal, 63*(3), 802–831.

Gurd, B., & Thomas, J. (2012). Family business management: Contribution of the CFO. *International Journal of Entrepreneurial Behaviour and Research, 18*(3), 286–304. https://doi.org/10.1108/13552551211227684

Habib, A., & Hasan, M. M. (2017). Social capital and corporate cash holdings. *International Review of Economics & Finance, 52*, 1–20. https://doi.org/10.1016/j.iref.2017.09.005

Hambrick, D. C., & Mason, P. A. (1984). Upper echelons: The organization as a reflection of its top managers. *Academy of Management Review, 9*(2), 193–206. https://doi.org/10.2307/258434

Hanek, K. J., Garcia, S. M., & Tor, A. (2016). Gender and competitive preferences: The role of competition size. *Journal of Applied Psychology, 101*(8), 1122. https://doi.org/10.1037/apl0000112

Hang, M., Geyer-Klingeberg, J., Rathgeber, A. W., & Stöckl, S. (2018). Measurement matters – A meta-study of the determinants of corporate capital structure. *The Quarterly Review of Economics and Finance, 68*(C), 211–225. https://doi.org/10.1016/j.qref.2017.11.011

Han, D., Liu, Q., Wei, Z., & Hao, Y. (2020). Are female CFOs trailblazers or sustainers? Evidence from industry growth prospects in China. *Asia-Pacific Journal of Accounting & Economics, 29*(4), 1–21. https://doi.org/10.1080/16081625.2020.1847150

Han, S. J., & Qiu, J. R. (2007). Corporate precautionary cash holdings. *Journal of Corporate Finance, 13*, 43–57. https://doi.org/10.1016/j.jcorpfin.2006.05.002

Harford, J., Mansi, S. A., & Maxwell, W. F. (2008). Corporate governance and firm cash holdings in the US. *Journal of Financial Economics, 87*, 535–555. https://doi.org/10.1016/j.jfineco.2007.04.002

Harjoto, M. A., Laksmana, I., & Yang, Y. W. (2018). Board diversity and corporate investment oversight. *Journal of Business Research, 90*, 40–47. https://doi.org/10.1016/j.jbusres.2018.04.033

Harris, C. K. (2014). Women directors on public company boards: Does a critical mass affect leverage? *Proceedings of the Northeastern Association of Business, Economics, and Technology* (Publication 29), 139–154. https://digitalcommons.ursinus.edu/bus_econ_fac/29/

Harrison, G. W., Lau, M. I., & Rutström, E. E. (2007). Estimating risk attitudes in Denmark: A field experiment. *The Scandinavian Journal of Economics, 109*(2), 341–368. https://doi.org/10.1111/j.1467-9442.2007.00496.x

Harris, M., & Raviv, A. (1991). The theory of capital structure. *The Journal of Finance, 46*(1), 297–355. https://doi.org/10.1111/j.1540-6261.1991.tb03753.x

Haushalter, D., Klasa, S., & Maxwell, W. F. (2007). The influence of product market dynamics on a Firm's cash holdings and hedging behaviour. *Journal of Financial Economics, 84*, 797–825. https://doi.org/10.1016/j.jfineco.2006.05.007

Haynes, K. T., & Hillman, A. (2010). The effect of board capital and CEO power on strategic change. *Strategic Management Journal, 31*(11), 1145–1163. https://doi.org/10.1002/smj.859

Hayward, M. L. A., & Hambrick, D. C. (1997). Explaining the premiums paid for large acquisitions: Evidence of CEO hubris. *Administrative Science Quarterly, 42*(1), 103–127. https://doi.org/10.2307/2393810

Hernandez, M. (2012). Toward an understanding of the psychology of stewardship. *The Academy of Management Review, 37*(2), 172–193. https://doi.org/10.5465/amr.2010.0363

Hernández-Nicolás, C. M., Martín-Ugedo, J. F., & Mínguez-Vera, A. (2019). The effect of gender diversity on the board of Spanish agricultural cooperatives on returns and debt: An empirical analysis. *Agribusiness, 35*(4), 639–656. https://doi.org/10.1002/agr.21608

Herrmann, P., & Datta, D. K. (2005). Relationships between top management team characteristics and international diversification: An empirical investigation. *British*

112   References

Journal of Management, 16(1), 69–78. https://doi.org/10.1111/j.1467-8551.2005. 00429.x

Hiebl, M. R. W. (2013a). Bean counter or strategist? Differences in the role of the CFO in family and non-family businesses. Journal of Family Business Strategy, 4(2), 147–161. https://doi.org/10.1016/j.jfbs.2013.02.003

Hiebl, M. R. W. (2013b). Non-family CFOs in family businesses: Do they fit? Journal of Business Strategy, 34(2), 45–51. https://doi.org/10.1108/02756661311310459

Hiebl, M. R. W. (2015). Agency and stewardship attitudes of chief financial officers in private companies. Qualitative Research in Financial Markets, 7(1), 4–23. https:// doi.org/10.1108/QRFM-12-2012-0032

Hillman, A. J., Canella, A. A., & Harris, I. C. (2002). Women and racial minorities in the boardroom: How do directors differ? Journal of Management, 28(6), 747–763. https://doi.org/10.1016/S0149-2063(02)00192-7

Hillson, D., & Murray-Webster, R. (2007). Understanding and managing risk attitude (2nd ed.). London: Routledge. https://doi.org/10.4324/9781315235448

Ho, S. S. M., Li, A. Y., Tam, K., & Zhang, F. (2015). CEO gender, ethical leadership, and accounting conservatism. Journal of Business Ethics, 127(2), 351–370. https:// doi.org/10.1007/s10551-013-2044-0

Hoitash, R., Hoitash, U., & Kurt, A. C. (2016). Do accountants make better chief financial officers? Journal of Accounting and Economics, 61(2–3), 414–432. https://doi. org/10.1016/j.jacceco.2016.03.002

Huang, J., & Kisgen, D. J. (2013), Gender and corporate finance: Are male executives overconfident relative to female executives? Journal of Financial Economics, 108(3), 822–839. https://doi.org/10.1016/j.jfineco.2012.12.005

Huang, S. Y., Tsaih, R. H., & Lin, W. Y. (2012). Unsupervised neural networks approach for understanding fraudulent financial reporting. Industrial Management & Data Systems, 112(2), 224–244. https://doi.org/10.1108/02635571211204272

Isidro, H., & Sobral, M. (2015). The effects of women on corporate boards on firm value, financial performance, and ethical and social compliance. Journal of Business Ethics, 132(1), 1–19. https://doi.org/10.1007/s10551-014-2302-9

Iskandar-Datta, M., & Shekhar, S. (2020). Do insider CFOs deliver better acquisition performance? Journal of Business Research, 118(C), 240–252. https://doi.org/ 10.1016/j.jbusres.2020.06.040

Javeed, S. A., & Lefen, L. (2019). An analysis of corporate social responsibility and firm performance with moderating effects of CEO power and ownership structure: A case study of the manufacturing sector of Pakistan. Sustainability, 11(1), 248. https:// doi.org/10.3390/su11010248

Jaworski, J., & Czerwonka, L. (2023). Która teoria struktury kapitału wyjaśnia decyzje finansowe małych i średnich przedsiębiorstw? Wyniki badań dotyczących Polski. Gospodarka Narodowa. The Polish Journal of Economics, 313(1), 82–92. https:// doi.org/10.33119/GN/159035

Jensen, M. C. (1986). Agency costs of free cash flow, corporate finance, and takeovers. The American Economic Review, 76(2), 323–329.

Jensen, M. C. (2010). Value maximization, stakeholder theory, and the corporate objective function. Journal of Applied Corporate Finance, 22(1), 32–42. https://doi. org/10.2307/3857812

Jensen, M. C., & Meckling, W. H. (1976). Theory of the firms: Managerial behavior, agency costs and ownership structure. Journal of Financial Economics, 3(4), 305–360. https://doi.org/10.1016/0304-405X(76)90026-X

Jiang, J., Petroni, K. R., & Wang, I. Y. (2010). CFOs and CEOs: Who has the most influence on earnings management? *Journal of Financial Economics*, *96*(3), 513–526. https://doi.org/10.1016/j.jfineco.2010.02.007

Johnson, D. L., & Qi, H. (2008). WACC misunderstandings. *The Journal of Financial Issues*, *6*(1), 32–40. https://doi.org/10.58886/jfi.v6i1.2432

Kagzi, M., & Guha, M. (2018). Board demographic diversity: A review of literature. *Journal of Strategy and Management*, *11*(1), 33–51. https://doi.org/10.1108/JSMA-01-2017-0002

Kai, C. Y. (1996). *The Scope of the Role of a Chief Financial Officer. A Study in Singapore Contex.* www3.ntu.edu.sg(05.04.2015).

Karpuś, P. (2006). Wprowadzenie do zarządzania finansami. In P. Karpuś (Ed.), *Zarządzanie finansami przedsiębiorstw* (pp. 13–59). Lublin: Wydawnictwo UMCS.

Keck, S., & Tang, W. (2016). Can powerful chief financial officers improve acquisition decisions? *Academy of Management Proceedings*, *2016*(1), 14142. https://doi.org/10.5465/ambpp.2016.14142abstract

Khalid, F., Naveed, K., He, X., & Ye, C. (2022). Impact of chief financial officer's experience on the assurance of corporate social responsibility reports in China. *Society and Business Review*, *17*(4), 613–635. https://doi.org/10.1108/SBR-10-2021-0190

Khan, A. N., Yahya, F., & Waqas, M. (2022). Board diversity and working capital management strategies: Evidence from energy sector of Pakistan. *Journal of Economic and Administrative Sciences*, ahead-of-print. https://doi.org/10.1108/JEAS-09-2021-0183

Kim, Y., & Cannella, A. A. Jr. (2008). Toward a social capital theory of director selection. *Corporate Governance: An International Review*, *16*(4), 282–293. https://doi.org/10.1111/j.1467-8683.2008.00693.x

Kim, H., & Lim, C. (2010). Diversity, outside directors and firm valuation: Korean evidence. *Journal of Business Research*, *63*(3), 284–291. https://doi.org/10.1016/j.jbusres.2009.01.013

Kirsch, A. (2018). The gender composition of corporate boards: A review and research agenda. *The Leadership Quarterly*, *29*(2), 346–364. https://doi.org/10.1016/j.leaqua.2017.06.001

Kolb, R. W., & Rodriguez, R. J. (1992). *Financial management.* Lexington: D. C. Heath and Company.

König, A. N. (2021). Domain-specific risk attitudes and aging—A systematic review. *Journal of Behavioral Decision Making*, *34*(3), 359–378. https://doi.org/10.1002/bdm.2215

Korkeamäki, T., Liljeblom, E., & Pasternack, D. (2017). CEO power and matching leverage preferences. *Journal of Corporate Finance*, *45*(C), 19–30. https://doi.org/10.1016/j.jcorpfin.2017.04.007

Kothari, S. P., Mizik, N., & Roychowdhury, S. (2016). Managing for the moment: The role of earnings management via real activities versus accruals in SEO valuation. *The Accounting Review*, *91*(2), 559–586. https://doi.org/10.2308/accr-51153

Koufopoulos, D., Zoumbos, V., Argyropoulou, M., & Motwani, J. (2008). Top management team and corporate performance: A study of Greek firms. *Team Performance Management*, *14*(7/8), 340–363. https://doi.org/10.1108/13527590810912322

Kramoliš, J., & Dobeš, K. (2020). Debt as a financial risk factor in SMEs in the Czech Republic. Equilibrium. *Quarterly Journal of Economics and Economic Policy*, *15*(1), 87–105. https://doi.org/10.24136/eq.2020.005

La Rocca, M., La Rocca, T., Stagliano, R., Vecellio, P., & Montalto, F. (2019). Gender diversity, cash holdings and the role of the institutional environment: Empirical evidence in Europe. *Applied Economics, 51*(29), 3137–3152. https://doi.org/10.1080/00036846.2019.1566687

Larwood, L., & Whittaker, W. (1977). Managerial myopia: Self-serving biases in organizational planning. *Journal of Applied Psychology, 62*(2), 194–198. https://doi.org/10.1037/0021-9010.62.2.194

Latham, S., & Braun, M. (2010). Does short-termism influence firm innovation? An examination of S&P 500 firms, 1990–2003. *Journal of Managerial Issues, 22,* 368–382.

Le Breton-Miller, I., Miller, D., & Lester, R. H. (2011). Stewardship or agency? A social embeddedness reconciliation of conduct and performance in public family businesses. *Organization Science, 22*(3), 704–721. https://doi.org/10.1287/orsc.1100.0541

Le, S., & Kroll, M. (2017). CEO international experience: Effects on strategic change and firm performance. *Journal of International Business Studies, 48*(5), 573–595. https://doi.org/10.1057/s41267-017-0080-1

Levi, Y., & Welch, I. (2017). Best practice for cost-of-capital estimates. *Journal of Financial and Quantitative Analysis, 52*(2), 427–463. https://doi.org/10.1017/S0022109017000114

Lewis, B. W., Walls, J. L., & Dowell, G. W. S. (2014). Difference in degrees: CEO characteristics and firm environmental disclosure. *Strategic Management Journal, 35*(5), 712–722. https://doi.org/10.1002/smj.2127

Lian, Y., Sepehri, M., & Foley, M. (2011). Corporate cash holdings and financial crisis: An empirical study of Chinese companies. Eurasian Business Review, *Eurasia Business and Economics Society, 1*(2), 112–124, https://doi.org/10.14208/BF03353801

Lin, S. W.-J., Liu, R., & Wang, C. (2014). Do CEOs pressure CFOs to manage earnings? (Working Paper). https://www.researchgate.net/publication/272165466_Do_CEOs_pressure_CFOs_to_manage_earnings

Lin, Y., Hu, S., & Chen, M. (2005). Managerial optimism and corporate investment: Some empirical evidence from Taiwan. *Pacific-Basin Finance Journal, 13*(5), 523–546. https://doi.org/10.1016/j.pacfin.2004.12.003

Liu, Y., Neely, P., & Karim, K. (2022). The impact of CFO gender on corporate overinvestment. *Advances in Accounting, 57*(October 2020), 100599. https://doi.org/10.1016/j.adiac.2022.100599

Liu, X., Yang, J., Di, R., & Li, M. (2022). CFO tenure and classification shifting: Evidence from China. *Emerging Markets Finance and Trade, 58*(6), 1578–1589. https://doi.org/10.1080/1540496X.2021.1904879

Luo, J. H., Peng, C., & Zhang, X. (2020). The impact of CFO gender on corporate fraud: Evidence from China. *Pacific-Basin Finance Journal, 63,* 101404. https://doi.org/10.1016/j.pacfin.2020.101404

Lutz, W., Cuaresma, J. C., & Abbasi-Shavazi, M. J. (2010). Demography, education, and democracy: Global trends and the case of Iran. *Population and Development Review, 36*(2), 253–281. http://dx.doi.org/10.1111/j.1728-4457.2010.00329.x

Lutz, E., & Schraml, S. (2012). Family firms: Should they hire an outside CFO? *Journal of Business Strategy, 33*(1), 39–44. https://doi.org/10.1108/02756661211193802

Mahadeo, J. D., Soobaroyen, T., & Hanuman, V. O. (2012). Board composition and financial performance: Uncovering the effects of diversity in an emerging economy. *Journal of Business Ethics, 105*(3), 375–388. https://doi.org/10.1007/s10551-011-0973-z

Malmendier, U., & Tate, G. (2005). CEO overconfidence and corporate investment. *Journal of Finance, 60*(6), 2261–2700. https://doi.org/10.1111/j.1540-6261.2005. 00813.x

Marinova, J., Plantenga, J., & Remery, C. (2016). Gender diversity and firm performance: Evidence from Dutch and Danish boardrooms. *International Journal of Human Resource Management, 27*(15), 1777–1790. https://doi.org/10.1080/09585192. 2015.1079229

Martino, P., Rigolini, A., & D'Onza, G. (2020). The relationships between CEO characteristics and strategic risk-taking in family firms. *Journal of Risk Research, 23*(1), 95–116. https://doi.org/10.1080/13669877.2018.1517380

Martín-Ugedo, J. F., & Minguez-Vera, A. (2014). Firm performance and women on the board: Evidence from the Spanish small and medium size companies. *Feminist Economics, 20*(3), 136–162.

Mellon, L., Nagel, D. C., Lippert, R., & Slack, N. (2012). *The new CFOs – How financial team and their leaders can revolutionize modern business.* London, UK and Philadelphia, PA: Kogan Page Publishers.

Mian, S. (2001). On the choice and replacement of chief financial officers. *Journals of Financial Economics, 60*(1), 143–175. https://doi.org/10.1016/S0304-405X(01)00042-3

Milliken, F. J., & Martins, L. L. (1996). Searching for common threads: Understanding the multiple effects of diversity in organizational groups. *Academy of Management Review, 21*(2), 402–433. https://doi.org/10.5465/amr.1996.9605060217

Mínguez-Vera, A., & Martin, A. (2011). Gender and management on Spanish SMEs: An empirical analysis. *The International Journal of Human Resource Management, 22*(14), 2852–2873. http://dx.doi.org/10.1080/09585192.2011.599948

Mirota, F., & Nehrebecka, N. (2018). Determinants of cash holdings in listed companies in Poland. *Gospodarka Narodowa. The Polish Journal of Economics, 295*(3), 75–102. https://doi.org/10.33119/GN/100489

Mishra, R. K., & Jhunjhunwala, S. (2013). *Diversity and the Effective Corporate Board.* Elsevier Monographs, Elsevier, edition 1, number 9780124104976.

Mobarek, A., Mollah, S., & Keasey, K. (2014). A cross-country analysis of herd behavior in Europe. *Journal of International Financial Markets, Institutions and Money, 32*, 107–127. https://doi.org/10.1016/j.intfin.2014.05.008

Mobbs, S. (2011). *Internal Financial Expertise on the Board: Implications of CFO board influence on firm financial policy* (SSRN Electronic Journal). http://dx.doi.org/10.2139/ssrn.1782959

Mobbs, S. (2018). Firm CFO board membership and departures. *Journal of Corporate Finance, 51*, 316–331. https://doi.org/10.1016/j.jcorpfin.2018.06.006

Modigliani, F., & Miller, M. H. (1963). Corporate income taxes and the cost of capital: A correction. *The American Economic Review, 53*(3), 433–443.

Molina, C. A. (2005). Are firms underleveraged? An examination of the effect of leverage on default probabilities. *The Journal of Finance, 60*(3), 1427–1459. http://dx.doi.org/10.1111/j.1540-6261.2005.00766.x

Morellec, E., & Schürhoff, N. (2011). Corporate investment and financing under asymmetric information. *Journal of Financial Economics, 99*(2), 262–288. https://doi.org/10.1016/j.jfineco.2010.09.003

Muttakin, M. B., Khan, A., & Tanewski, G. (2019). CFO tenure, CFO board membership and accounting conservatism. *Journal of Contemporary Accounting and Economics, 15*(3), 100165. https://doi.org/10.1016/j.jcae.2019.100165

Myers, S. C. (1984). The capital structure puzzle. *The Journal of Finance, 39,* 574–592. https://doi.org/10.1111/j.1540-6261.1984.tb03646.x

Myers, S. C., & Majluf, N. S. (1984). Corporate financing and investment decisions when firms have information that investors do not have. *Journal of Financial Economics, 13*(2), 187–221. https://doi.org/10.1016/0304-405X(84)90023-0

Naranjo-Gil, D., Maas, V. S., & Hartmann, F. G. (2009). How CFOs determine management accounting innovation: An examination of direct and indirect effects. *European Accounting Review, 18*(4), 667–695. http://dx.doi.org/10.1080/09638180802627795

Nastiti, P. K. Y., Atahau, A. D. R., & Supramono, S. (2020). Working capital management policy: Female top managers and firm profitability. *Journal of Management and Business Administration. Central Europe, 27*(3), 107–127. https://doi.org/10.7206/cemj.2658-0845.5

Nasution, D., & Jonnergård, K., (2017). Do auditor and CFO gender matter to earnings quality? Evidence from Sweden. *Gender in Management: An International Journal, 32*(5), 330–351. https://doi.org/10.1108/GM-06-2016-0125

Naumoski, A., & Bucevska, V. (2022). Impact of company-specific determinants on corporate cash holdings: Evidence from South-East European countries. *Scientific Papers of the* University of Pardubice, Series D: Faculty of Economics and Administration, *30*(2), 1554, http://hdl.handle.net/20.500.12188/24400

Nielsen, S. (2010). Top management team diversity: A review of theories and methodologies. *International Journal of Management Reviews, 12*(3), 301–316. https://doi.org/10.1111/j.1468-2370.2009.00263.x

Ojeka, S. A., Adegboye, A., Adegboye, K., Alabi, O., Afolabi, M., & Iyoha, F. (2019). Chief financial officer roles and enterprise risk management: An empirical based study. *Heliyon, 5*(6), e01934. https://doi.org/10.1016/j.heliyon.2019.e01934

Opler, T., Pinkowitz, L., Stulz, R., & Williamson, R. (1999). The determinants and implications of corporate cash holdings. *Journal of Financial Economics, 52*(1), 3–46. https://doi.org/10.1016/S0304-405X(99)00003-3

Orens, R., & Reheul, A. M. (2013). Do CEO demographics explain cash holdings in SMEs? *European Management Journal, 31*(6), 549–563. https://doi.org/10.1016/j.emj.2013.01.003

Panda, B., & Leepsa, N. M. (2017). Agency theory: Review of theory and evidence on problems and perspectives. *Indian Journal of Corporate Governance, 10*(1), 74–95. https://doi.org/10.1177/0974686217701467

Pauka, M., & Żyła, M. (2018). Performance signalling of dividend policy on the NewConnect market. *Annales Universitatis Mariae Curie-Skłodowska, Sectio H– Oeconomia, 51*(6), 301–309. http://dx.doi.org/10.17951/h.2017.51.6.301.

Pavlatos, O., & Kostakis, X. (2018). The impact of top management team characteristics and historical financial performance on strategic management accounting. *Journal of Accounting & Organizational Change, 14,* 455–472. https://doi.org/10.1108/JAOC-11-2017-0112

Peltomäki, J., Sihvonen, J., Swidler, S., & Vähämaa, S. (2021). Age, gender, and risk-taking: Evidence from the S&P 1500 executives and market-based measures of firm risk. *Journal of Business Finance and Accounting, 48*(9–10), 1988–2014. https://doi.org/10.1111/jbfa.12528

Pfeffer, J., & Salancik, G. (1978). The *external control of organizations: A resource dependence perspective.* Stanford, CT: Harper & Row.

Pilbeam, K..(2010). *Finance & financial market*. London: Palgrave Macmillan.

Pinkowitz, L., Stulz, R. M., & Williamson, R. (2013). Is there a US high cash holdings puzzle after the financial crisis? Fisher College of Business (Working Paper) No. 2013-03-07.

Portes, A. (1998). Social capital: Its origins and applications in modern sociology. *Annual Review of Sociology*, *24*, 1–24. https://doi.org/10.1146/annurev.soc. 24.1.1

Puri, M., & Robinson, D. T. (2007). Optimism and economic choice. *Journal of Financial Economics*, *86*(1), 71–99. https://doi.org/10.1016/j.jfineco.2006.09.003

Qi, B., & Tian, G. (2012). The impact of audit committees personal characteristics on earnings management: Evidence from China. *Journal of Applied Business Research (JABR)*, *28*(6), 1331–1344. https://doi.org/10.19030/jabr.v28i6.7347

Ran, G., Fang, Q., Luo, S., & Chan, K. C. (2015). Supervisory board characteristics and accounting information quality: Evidence from China. *International Review of Economics and Finance*, *37*, 18–32. https://doi.org/10.1016/j.iref.2014.10.011

Ross, S. A., Westerfield, R. W., & Jordan, B. D. (1993). *Fundamentals of corporate finance*. Boston: McGraw-Hill/Irwin.

Rossi, F., Cebula, R. J., & Barth, J. R. (2018). Female representation in the boardroom and firm debt: Empirical evidence from Italy. *Journal of Economics and Finance*, *42*(2), 315–338. https://doi.org/10.1007/s12197-017-9397-7

Rubin, S. J. (2017). *The Relationship Between a CFO's Financial Expertise and Firm Profitability* (Publication No. 4480) [Walden Dissertations and Doctoral Studies, Walden University]. https://scholarworks.waldenu.edu/dissertations/4480

Sah, N. B., Adhikari, H. P., Krolikowski, M. W., Malm, J., & Nguyen, T. T. (2022). CEO gender and risk aversion: Further evidence using the composition of firm's cash. *Journal of Behavioral and Experimental Finance*, *33*, 100595. https://doi.org/ 10.1016/j.jbef.2021.100595

Schmid, S., & Altfeld, F. (2018). International work experience and compensation: Is more always better for CFOs? *European Management Journal*, *36*(4), 530–543.

Schopohl, L., Urquhart, A., & Zhang, H. (2021). Female CFOs, leverage and the moderating role of board diversity and CEO power. *Journal of Corporate Finance*, *71*(November 2020), 101858. https://doi.org/10.1016/j.jcorpfin.2020.101858

Seierstad, C. (2016). Beyond the business case: The need for both utility and justice rationales for increasing the share of women on boards. *Corporate Governance: An International Review*, *24*(4), 390–405. https://doi.org/10.1111/corg.12117

Sharma, R., & Jones, S. (2010). CFO of the future: Strategic contributor or value adder? *Journal of Applied Management Accounting Research*, *8*(1), 1–15.

Shehata, N., Salhin, A., & El-Helaly, M. (2017). Board diversity and firm performance: Evidence from the U.K. SMEs. *Applied Economics*, *49*(48), 4817–4832. https://doi. org/10.1080/00036846.2017.1293796

Sheikh, S. (2019). An examination of the dimensions of CEO power and corporate social responsibility. *Review of Accounting and Finance*, *18*(2), 221–244. https://doi. org/10.1108/RAF-01-2018-0034

Shleifer, A., & Vishny, R. W. (1997). A survey of corporate governance. *The Journal of Finance*, *52*, 737–783. https://doi.org/10.1111/j.1540-6261.1997.tb04820.x

Simionescu, L. N., Gherghina, Ş. C., Tawil, H., & Sheikha, Z. (2021). Does board gender diversity affect firm performance? Empirical evidence from standard & Poor's 500 information technology sector. *Financial Innovation*, *7*(1), 1–45. https://doi. org/10.1186/s40854-021-00265-x

Singh, H. P., Kumar, S., & Colombage, S. (2017). Working capital management and firm profitability: A meta-analysis. *Qualitative Research in Financial Markets, 9*(1), 34–47. https://doi.org/10.1108/QRFM-06-2016-0018

Sun, L., & Rakhman, F. (2013). CFO financial expertise and corporate social responsibility: Evidence from S&P 500 companies. *International Journal of Law and Management, 55*(3), 161–172. https://doi.org/10.1108/17542431311327619

Tajfel, H., & Turner, J. C. (1979). An integrative theory of intergroup conflict. In W. G. Austin, & S. Worchel (Eds.), *The social psychology of intergroup relations* (pp. 33–37). Monterey, CA: Brooks/Cole.

Tajfel, H., & Turner, J. C. (1986). The social identity theory of intergroup behavior. In S. Worchel, & W. G. Austin (Eds.), *Psychology of intergroup relation* (pp. 7–24). Chicago: Hall Publishers.

Talavera, O., Yin, S., & Zhang, M. (2018). Age diversity, directors' personal values, and bank performance. *International Review of Financial Analysis, 55,* 60–79. https://doi.org/10.1016/j.irfa.2017.10.007

Terjesen, S., Couto, E. B., & Francisco, P. M. (2016). Does the presence of independent and female directors impact firm performance? A multi-country study of board diversity. *Journal of Management and Governance, 20*(3), 447–483. https://doi.org/10.1007/s10997-014-9307-8

Tosun, O. K., El Kalak, I., & Hudson, R. (2022). How female directors help firms to attain optimal cash holdings. *International Review of Financial Analysis, 80,* 102034. https://doi.org/10.1016/j.irfa.2022.102034

Troy, C., Smith, K. G., & Domino, M. A. (2011). CEO demographics and accounting fraud: Who is more likely to rationalize illegal acts? *Strategic Organization, 9*(4), 259–282. https://doi.org/10.1177/1476127011421534

Turner, J. C. (1985). Social categorization and the self-concept: A social cognitive theory of group behaviour. In E. J. Lawler (Ed.), *Advances in group processes* (pp. 77–122). Greenwich, CT: JAI Press.

Velte, P. (2020). Corporate social responsibility and earnings management: A literature review. *Corporate Ownership & Control, 17*(2), 8–19. https://doi.org/10.22495/cocv17i2art1

Wawryszuk-Misztal, A. (2021a). *Finansowe czynniki i konsekwencje różnicowania składu osobowego zarządów i rad nadzorczych polskich spółek publicznych.* Lublin: Wydawnictwo UMCS.

Wawryszuk-Misztal, A. (2021b). Determinants of board diversity policy implementation by companies listed on the Warsaw stock exchange. *Equilibrium. Quarterly Journal of Economics and Economic Policy, 16*(3), 617–637. https://doi.org/10.24136/eq.2021.022

Wawryszuk-Misztal, A., & Wrońska-Bukalska, E. (2014). Duties of financial director from Board's perspective. In *Human capital without borders: Knowledge and learning for quality of life.* Proceedings of the Management Knowledge and Learning International Conference 2014 (pp. 673–680). Bangkok, Celje, Lublin: To Know Press, International Academic Publisher. http://www.toknowpress.net/ISBN/978-961-6914-09-3/papers/ML14-614.pdf

Weiss, Y. (2015). Gary Becker on human capital. *Journal of Demographic Economics, 81*(1), 27–31. https://doi.org/10.1017/dem.2014.4

Wen, W., Cui, H., & Ke, Y. (2020). Directors with foreign experience and corporate tax avoidance. *Journal of Corporate Finance, 62,* 101624.

Whitley, R. (1986). The transformation of business finance into financial economics: The roles of academic expansion and changes in U.S. *capital markets, Accounting, Organizations and Society, 11*(2), 171–192. https://doi.org/10.1016/0361-3682(86)90029-2

Wiersema, M. F., & Bantel, K. A. (1992). Top management team demography and corporate strategic change. *Academy of Management Journal, 35*(1), 91–121. https://doi.org/10.5465/256474

Wrońska-Bukalska, E. (2016). Overconfidence of Students and Managers - Comparative Analysis. *Proceedings of the 6th Economic and Finance Conferences,* International Institute of Social and Economic Sciences, OECD Headquarters, Paris. 349–361. https://doi.org/10.20472/EFC.2016.006.019

Xiong, J. (2016). Chairman characteristics and earnings management: Evidence from Chinese listed firms. *Open Journal of Accounting, 5,* 82–94. https://doi.org/10.4236/ojacct.2016.54008

Xu, X., Li, W., Li, Y., & Liu, X. (2019). Female CFOs and corporate cash holdings: Precautionary motive or agency motive? *International Review of Economics and Finance, 63*(May), 434–454. https://doi.org/10.1016/j.iref.2019.05.006

Zaid, M. A. A., Wang, M., Abuhijleh, S. T. F., Issa, A., Saleh, M. W. A., & Ali, F. (2020). Corporate governance practices and capital structure decisions: The moderating effect of gender diversity. *Corporate Governance (Bingley), 20*(5), 939–964. https://doi.org/10.1108/CG-11-2019-0343

Zalata, A. M., Ntim, C., Aboud, A., & Gyapong, E. (2022). Female CEOs and core earnings quality: New evidence on the ethics versus risk-aversion puzzle. *Business and the Ethical Implications of Technology, 160*(2), 209–228. https://doi.org/10.1007/s10551-018-3918-y

Zeng, S., & Wang, L. (2015). CEO gender and corporate cash holdings. Are female CEOs more conservative? *Asia-Pacific Journal of Accounting and Economics, 22*(4), 449–474. https://doi.org/10.1080/16081625.2014.1003568

Zorn, D. M. (2004). Here a chief, there a chief: The rise of the CFO in the American firm. *American Sociological Review, 69*(3), 345–364. https://doi.org/10.1177/000312240406900302

Index

For Product Safety Concerns and Information please contact our EU
representative GPSR@taylorandfrancis.com
Taylor & Francis Verlag GmbH, Kaufingerstraße 24, 80331 München, Germany